FRIENDS & FRIENDSHIP

Vol. 2 – REST OF THE WORLD

THE POET
Summer 2021

Compiled by Robin Barratt

THE POET

A leading international online poetry magazine, recognized for both
its quarterly themed collections, and its interviews with poets
worldwide; looking at their work and their words, and what motivates
and inspires them to write.

Interviews, profiles, articles, quarterly collections, Poet of the Week,
Poetry Courses and Young Poets.

www.ThePoetMagazine.org

~

FRIENDS & FRIENDSHIP
Vol.2 – REST OF THE WORLD

Published by THE POET

ISBN: 9798538072590

© THE POET, July2021, and all the authors herein

E: Robin@ThePoetMagazine.org

Cover image and design: Canva
www.Canva.com

Compiled and published for THE POET by:
Robin Barratt Publishing

Affordable Publishing Services

www.RobinBarratt.co.uk

THE POET is sponsored by:

www.PoemsOverCoffee.com

"John Johnson is a proud sponsor of THE POET."

If you would also like to sponsor THE POET, please go to:

www.thepoetmagazine.org/support-us

THANK YOU!

THANK YOU TO EVERYONE, EVERYWHERE SUPPORTING THE POET; WITHOUT YOUR HELP WE WOULDN'T BE ABLE TO CONTINUE SHOWCASING INSPIRING POETS AND PUBLISHING AMAZING POETRY ...

... AND WHAT A DULL WORLD THAT WOULD BE!

Love poetry?

Please support or sponsor us too; we are a not-for-profit, so everything goes back into showcasing poets and promoting poetry from around the world.

Go to the website for further details:

www.ThePoetMagazine.org

OTHER COLLECTIONS FROM THE POET

FAITH
With 234 contributions from 151 poets in 36 countries, and from 30 states in the US; published in two volumes, FAITH is probably one of the largest and most significant international collections of poetry on the theme of faith ever published.
Vol. 1 - USA – ISBN: 9798740844695
Vol. 2 - REST OF THE WORLD – ISBN: 9798740924557

CHILDHOOD
With over 300 contributions from 152 poets in 33 countries worldwide, and across 28 States in the USA, CHILDHOOD is in two volumes and is our most popular collection to date.
Vol. 1 - USA - ISBN: 9798564862332
Vol. 2 – REST OF THE WORLD - ISBN: 9798593564696

CHRISTMAS
With over 150 contributions from 97 poets in 34 countries, CHRISTMAS is probably one of the largest international anthologies of Christmas poetry ever published.
153 poems / 275 pages.
ISBN: 9798564859837

A NEW WORLD - Rethinking our lives post-pandemic.
Sixty-seven poets from around the world all writing on the theme of A NEW WORLD, exploring life post-pandemic.
115 poems/225 pages
ISBN: 9798696477084

SUMMER 2020 – ON THE ROAD Volumes 1 & 2
With one hundred and twenty poets from around the world, ON THE ROAD, is probably one of the largest international anthologies of travel poetry ever published.
Vol.1: 135 poems / 240 pages
ISBN: 9798640673593
Vol. 2: 117 poems / 245 pages
ISBN: 9798665956312

SPRING 2020 – WAR & BATTLE
Fifty-four poets from around the world all writing on the theme of WAR & BATTLE.
103 poems/215 pages.
ISBN: 9798629604594

WINTER 2019 - THE SEASONS
Thirty-four poets from around the world all writing on the theme of
THE SEASONS.
80 poems/129 pages.
ISBN: 9798600084445

AUTUMN 2019 - LOVE
THE POET's very first collection. Twenty-nine poets from around the
world all writing on the theme of LOVE.
73 poems/119 pages.
ISBN: 9781699169612

CONTENTS

13. Germain Droogenbroodt - SPAIN / BELGIUM
15. Richard Lister - ENGLAND
19. Stephen Kingsnorth - WALES
23. Ali Alhazmi - SAUDI ARABIA
25. Bill Cox - SCOTLAND
27. Zbigniew Roth - POLAND
29. Sultana Raza - LUXEMBOURG / INDIA
33. Francis H. Powell - ENGLAND
35. Bronwyn Vanzino - AUSTRALIA
37. Jyotirmaya Thakur - ENGLAND / INDIA
39. Hussein Habasch - KURDISTAN / GERMANY
43. Shweta Shanker - INDIA / SWITZERLAND
45. Pavol Janik, PhD - SLOVAKIA
49. William Khalipwina Mpina - MALAWI
53. Irma Kurti - ITALY / ALBANIA
57. Jojji Kaka - KENYA
61. Shikdar Mohammed Kibriah - BANGLADESH
63. Kate Meyer-Currey - ENGLAND
65. Rezauddin Stalin - BANGLADESH
69. Marian Dunham - ENGLAND
71. Jude Brigley - WALES
75. Danielle Holian - REPUBLIC OF IRELAND
79. Eliza Segiet - POLAND
81. Andrija Radulovic - MONTENEGRO
83. Alun Robert - ENGLAND
87. Sandesh Ghimire - NEPAL
89. Cheryl-lya Broadfoot - ENGLAND
93. John Notley - THAILAND / ENGLAND
95. Mahrukh Asmat - PAKISTAN
97. Yi Jung Chen - TAIWAN
99. Zorica Bajin Djukanovic - SERBIA
103. Onoruoiza Mark Onuchi - NIGERIA
107. Margaret Macdonald - SCOTLAND
109. Srimayee Gangopadhyay - INDIA
111. Nupur Shah - INDIA
115. Sunitha Srinivas C - INDIA
117. Veda Varma - KINGDOM OF BAHRAIN / INDIA
121. Rema Tabangcura - PHILIPPINES / SINGAPORE
123. Kristine Ventura - MALAYSIA / PHILIPPINES
125. Aminath Neena - MALDIVES
131. Kate Young - ENGLAND
133. Aleksandra Vujisić - MONTENEGRO
137. Zana Coven - ITALY

139. David Hollywood - REPUBLIC OF IRELAND
141. Mark Andrew Heathcote - ENGLAND
143. Sam Eastwood - NEW ZEALAND
147. Xanthi Hondrou-Hill - GREECE
151. Achingliu Kamei - INDIA
153. Jenny Brown - ENGLAND
157. Masudul Hoq - BANGLADESH
159. Prafull Shiledar - INDIA
161. Igor Pop Trajkov - REPUBLIC OF NORTH MACEDONIA
165. Rosy Gallace - ITALY
169. Suchismita Ghoshal - INDIA
173. Shaswata Gangopadhyay - INDIA
175. Arpita Sam - BAHRAIN / INDIA
177. Chrys Salt MBE - ENGLAND / SCOTLAND
179. Eduard Schmidt-Zorner - REPUBLIC OF IRELAND / GERMANY
181. Rodavgi Gkogkoni - GREECE
183. Maid Čorbić - BOSNIA AND HERZEGOVINA
185. Daniela Andonovska-Trajkovska - REPUBLIC OF NORTH MACEDONIA
187. Borche Panov - REPUBLIC OF NORTH MACEDONIA
189. Anna Banasiak - POLAND
191. Ewith Bahar - INDONESIA
193. Jean E. Ragual - SINGAPORE / PHILIPPINES
195. Jelena Zagorac - SERBIA
197. Meenakshi Palaniappan - SINGAPORE
201. Gabriella Garofalo - ITALY
205. Lindsay Walter - ENGLAND
209. Keith Jepson - ENGLAND
211. Glória Sofia - CAPE VERDE
213. Dr. Eftichia Kapardeli - GREECE
215. Monica Manolachi - ROMANIA
217. Amrita Valan - INDIA
219. Lorraine Sicelo Mangena - ZIMBABWE
221. Janelyn Dupingay Vergara - SINGAPORE / PHILIPPINES
223. Kathleen Boyle - VIETNAM / ENGLAND
225. Heera Nawaz - INDIA
227. John Tunaley - ENGLAND
229. Naicy Candido - SINGAPORE / PHILIPPINES
231. Melissa Nazareth - KINGDOM OF BAHRAIN
233. Michelle Morris - ENGLAND
235. Marilyn Longstaff - ENGLAND
237. Máire Malone - ENGLAND / REPUBLIC OF IRELAND
239. Shagun Shukla - INDIA
243. Ergasheva Mashhura - UZBEKISTAN
245. Prof. Jeton Kelmendi - KOSOVO / BELGIUM
249. Kathleen Bleakley - AUSTRALIA

251. Amelia Fielden - AUSTRALIA
253. Nivedita Karthik - INDIA
257. Anamika Nandy - INDIA
259. Suranjit Gain - BANGLADESH
261. Ailenemae Salvador - HONG KONG / PHILIPPINES
263. Jennifer Sisasenkosi Chiveya - ZIMBABWE
265. Manju Kanchuli Tiwari - NEPAL
269. Elisabetta Bagli - SPAIN / ITALY
273. Ankita Patel - INDIA
277. Ndaba Sibanda - ZIMBABWE / ETHIOPIA
279. Rozalia Aleksandrova - BULGARIA
283. Daniela Marian - ROMANIA
285. Madhavi Tiwary - KINGDOM OF BAHRAIN / INDIA
287. Mónika Tóth - ROMANIA
289. Maria Nemy Lou Rocio - HONG KONG / PHILIPPINES
293. Audrey Savage - ENGLAND
295. Barbara Webb - ENGLAND
299. Barbra Dean - SPAIN / ENGLAND
301. Dr. Sarah Clarke - KINGDOM OF BAHRAIN

FRIENDS
noun

a person attached to another by feelings of affection
or personal regard.

a person who is on good terms with another;
a person who is not hostile.

FRIENDSHIP
noun

the state of being a friend; association as friends.

to value a person's friendship.

a friendly relation or intimacy.

friendly feeling or disposition.

www.Dictionary.com

Germain Droogenbroodt
SPAIN / BELGIUM

Germain Droogenbroodt is an internationally appreciated poet, translator, publisher and promoter of modern international poetry. He wrote short stories and literary reviews, but mainly poetry, so far 14 poetry books, published in 19 countries. As founder of the Belgian publishing house POINT *Editions* he published more than eighty collections of mainly modern, international poetry. He organised and co-organised several international poetry festivals in Spain, is vice president of the Academy Mihai Eminescu, in Romania, co-founder and advisor of JUNPA (Japan Universal Poets Association), artistic advisor of the Italian movement Poetry & Discovery, and founding president of the Spanish cultural foundation ITHACA. He also set up the internationally greatly appreciated project Poetry without Borders, publishing every week a poem from all over the world in 29 languages. Several famous artists made paintings and sculptures inspired by his poetry, and international composers composed music to his poems. He visited countless times the Far East and studied Chinese philosophy which inspired his poetry, TAO pretend Chinese which greatly appreciate and published his poetry in China, Hong Kong and Taiwan. Japanese pretend his poetry is ZEN, four of his poetry books have been published in Japan, including a collection of haiku. Germain has received more than a dozen international poetry awards as poet and as promoter of international poetry, and every year is invited to give recitals and conferences at universities and at the most prestigious international poetry festivals. He was nominated for the Nobel prize in Literature 2017.
E: elpoeta@point-editions.com
W: www.point-editions.com

A GLEAM OF LIGHT

In the eyes
a glister of moonlight
a soft breeze
like sometimes a word
a hand gesture
or an embrace
a glimmer of light,
things for the heart.

Richard Lister
ENGLAND

Richard lives in the beautiful Surrey Hills near Dorking. He takes you into the stories of intriguing people, cultures and places. He draws on his experience of living and working in Cambodia during an ongoing conflict, in the jungles of Belize and in Malawi, a country known as 'The Warm Heart of Africa'. He works as a coach and mentor for leaders, and enables communities to move out of poverty across Africa, Asia and Latin America. As a semi-abstract painter, Richard writes with an artist's eye for the visually evocative. He's a Mole Valley Poet and member of Ros Barber's Poetry School workshops and Writing for Wellbeing. Richard's work has been carved into the Radius Sculpture, exhibited in The Fading of the Light Exhibition, and published in Only in the Shadow, Home and South Magazine. His book Flourish: full life for all will be published in December 2021.
E: richardnwlister@gmail.com

YOU ARE A DEVON COVE
For Nic

a beach gifted with slate
by the bluster of the waves.

You are a stream that
lays down each grain
of sand with care.

You are a crevice
filled with shadows
and pirate's coin.

You are a rockpool
open to be a cupped
stretch of the sea.

You are a rock strung
with limpets of limestone,
trench and parterre.

You are a storm blasting
the trashers of land,
the fools and their dogs.

You are the wind
whispered with words carved
from traveller's tales.

You are Aymers Cove, unique
and wondrously made,
a friend through the hail and the rain.

A PEW, A PILLAR AND YOU
For Nic

I clutch what I want to say.
Note my stomach tense
with fear that I'll slip
into silence like a trout drifting
with the flow into the shallows.
'I have a voice. Hear me!'

So, as we climb the lane,
I share that I've written
Chapter 8 of Flourish,
started Lead like a Fish,
divided my poems by theme.
Precious but self-burnished.

The air is stung with cold,
the light, cut grey as if the sun
has drifted south and out of sight.
Hawthorn blossoms
have lost their fiery lustre
and blackthorn may never bud.

You can tell the thorns apart,
discern the Black Cap's warble
and know that Beeching's Cuts
brought the railway line,
set up for ten-coached trains,
to weed-strewn, trackless sleep.

We knock sparks from the flints
of our knowledge, the collapse
of the siege of Orléans giving rise
to French identity. Nationalism's
seductive words. Lord Gray's
fumbled nuance. The Great War.

And find ourselves at either end
of a honeyed walnut pew in St Johns.
I am leaning against a pillar, idling my eyes
over the arched fingers of the roof
and starting to share into the unhurried space
you hold. It's *hard*, my precious wife's

Long Covid. *It seems cruel,*
after a decade of chronic fatigue,
stomach migraines and loss
she had a clear call to priesthood,
yet those spring shoots
have not survived the frost.

As I slow and dare to speak,
my crafted poetic words fail
and all that's left is me
with common pain, tears
behind my eyes and you, my friend.
A pew, a pillar and you.

Stephen Kingsnorth

WALES

Stephen (Cambridge M.A., English & Religious Studies), born in London, retired to Wales from ministry in the Methodist Church with Parkinson's Disease, has had some 300 pieces published by on-line poetry sites, printed journals and anthologies, most recently *Academy of the Heart and Mind, The Parliament Literary Magazine, Runcible Spoon,* and *Poetry Potion*.
E: slkingsnorth@googlemail.com
W: www.poetrykingsnorth.wordpress.com

HIVE

The ukulele, not best for Danny Boy,
means unaccompanied, we gravel to begin;
our chariot choir sings high and low,
though jointly note the middle range.

Despite harmonious melody,
the Dublin-born disputes the tune
is Londonderry Air, an Ulster name.
But with Guinness I have heard
plantation words alongside craic,
and Prot bars resound republican.
We warble words with the chorus girls,
a hurting leg, Jack's grunt refrain.

Out the door, politics; here we laugh
at wheelchair three point-turn or six
in this space, confined, it's like
our repartee, the discourse of humanity,
Areopagus of fun.

Kim, the crochet girl has brought a bag
of kitchenalia to identify.
This largely plastic crowded tray
whets few appetites today.

With glove stretchers, I had never need
of tongs to empty sauce sachets,
or the mango stone remover,
the sandwich cutter which prevents
squashed jam seeping from bread edges.
Yesterday sachets and mangoes
were not in the scullery,
or indeed between my teeth,
while butter or jam were choice,
and crustiness, grandpa's trait,
an ingredient of life.

Because the baby has been born
half-knit blue cardigan
has sleeves now turning pink;
desultory chair exercise
brings the needles overhead.

This group, hive christened,
and we its bees;
some come from ever-silent rooms
and travel here without sound,
broken-winged, as if the sting
already taken from our tale.

Once my thought-question
slipped from lips;
it might have searched opinions,
we could have shared spoken debate,
we might have made a meal of it.
But when the leader googles phone,
the answer served on a plate,
then beehive becomes an igloo still,
snake-charmer's basket on its head,
and honey comb cannot mature.

The yellow high-viz jacket wears
a button hole, woollen daffodil,
but insists it to be a crocus flower.
In stitches
he offers me its curling bloom to smell;
we are back to buzzing
and that perfume claims the room.

First published by *Eunoia Review*, 6th September, 2019.

RATIONED

I'm hungry for those former days
when life made sense, friends' names were known;
I recognised my family then,
now introduce themselves again.
I find my bed, black tiles on pink,
blank corridors, dust free, pristine,
cleared well meant, old directing junk;
my appetite, Dad's frame, askew.
I'm starved of words that sprang to sound,
play hide and seek, but rarely found,
on tongue tip where taste buds declined,
now buried, lexigrave of mind.

I sit for pudding, porridge served,
bring breakfast when desert arrives,
and salad now my cocoa mug,
rash napkin whetted, terry style.
Then read incunabula, tracts
now tablets swallowed, infections,
and soaps, hers lilac, mine coal tar,
soak from their airing, cupboard screen.
I hear the music, early spheres,
the dance hall, disco, swinging years,
those Sunday tunes when singing hymns,
whose rhythms breathe, pull heartfelt strings.

Ali Alhazmi
SAUDI ARABIA

Born in Damadd, Saudi Arabia, Ali Alhazmi obtained a degree in Arabic Language and Literature at Umm Al-Qura University, Faculty of Arabic Language. As early as 1985, Ali started publishing his poetry in a variety of local and Arabic international cultural publications including *The Seventh Day* (Paris), *Creativity* (Cairo), *Nazoa* (Amman) and *The New Text*. He has participated various International Poetry Festivals including; Costa Rica (2013), Spain (2014), Uruguay (2015), Cuba, Colombia and Turkey (2016), Italy and Romania (2017) and Spain (2018). His work has been translated into many languages, and his publications include: *A Gate for the Body* (1993), *Loss* (2000), *Deer Drink Its Own Image* (2004), *Comfortable on the Edge* (2009), and *Now in the Past* (2018). His awards include: Medal of Poetry (Uruguay, 2015), The World Grand Prize for Poetry, (Romania 2017), the Verbumlandi Prize (Italy, 2017) and Best International Poet (China, 2018).
E: ali-alhazmi@hotmail.com
FB: @Alhazmi.ali

DEPARTURE

At airports,
Roses of words dry up so rapidly;
Birds of the eyes, falling upon the terraces of the faces, Address the
verses of their purity in bitter longing;
Icy fingers melt in the warm hands,
Grasping the last wishes,
For the last time.
Leather bags of sadness seem ready for vomiting
Upon hearing the last call.
Hands urge the tears to fall down from the sublime trees Blooming in
the ribs.
Hearts depart the bodies of dear persons
On seats about to fly.
A nectar of kisses travelling on a cheek
That has already fastened the safety belt to its waist. A river of chaos
mingles with cries
Swimming in the whiteness of their conscience,
And wastes the last minutes of quick last hugs
On a receding shore.
Since distances are diminishing in the eyes dreaming of a similar
flight, The roses of words will stay on the airport floor,
Lifeless and dried up, In complete despair.

Bill Cox
SCOTLAND

Bill was born and bred in 'the Granite City' of Aberdeen, Scotland and he currently lives there with his partner Hilary, and their grown-up baby daughter Catherine. Bill enjoyed creative writing when at school, but as the cliché goes, life got in the way and it was only in his forties, after taking an online course, that he returned to his teenage passion. He now writes for the sheer enjoyment of it, which is just as well as no-one seems willing to pay him to do it. He dabbles mainly in poetry and short fiction, as he hasn't built up the stamina yet to write anything longer. One day, though, he plans to gather his strength and write a book that will set the publishing world alight. In the meantime he satisfies himself with composing bawdy limericks in his head.

E: malphesius@yahoo.com
W: www.northeastnotesblog.wordpress.com

FRIENDS

Hobby friends, that share my passion,
Shopping friends, for the latest fashion.
School friends, chums for life,
Lover and friend, that's the wife.
Coffee friends, sharing the news,
Musician friends, playing the Blues.
Facebook friends that read my posts,
Pub friends, who indulge my boasts.
Gym friends, for working out,
Fishing friends, for catching trout.
Work friends, make the office fun,
Dog friends, best pals bar none.
Friends who'll help me move,
Friends who are in my groove,
Friends who drive me round the bend,
Friends till the bitter end.
Without a friend a day seems empty,
They are the source of life's sweet plenty.
They are all life's dividend,
Which is why I'm proud to call you,
Friend.

Zbigniew Roth
POLAND

Zbigniew is an author, composer and poet; he has been writing since 1957, and composing since 1968. He is a Critic Correspondent and Journalist in the field of Poetry and Song for Polish-Italian TV News, the President and Founder of the SSAP World Association of Artists and Writers, and is a member of a large number of international literary groups and organisations including: the Polish American Poets Academy, the Literary and Dramatic Group, the 83 Infrared Circle, the Polish Association of Authors, Journalists and Translators, the the Polish Society of Artists, Authors, Cultural Animators.
E: poezja.muzyka.sport@gmail.com
FB: @serce.poezja

SONG OF THE UNITED NATIONS

this is our common home
and there are continents in it
you and I live on them
we all have common dreams

the sun shines in the desert
on flowery meadows too
even where the frost is eternal
and where it often rains

love doesn't know any races
and works well in a difficult time
it doesn't matter what you believe
when a neighbour lies sick

this house is for all of us
where people tremble because of people
give me a hand against pain, protect me
be helpful when others want it

believe in yourself also in people
turn words into deeds in a common song
it is a brotherhood of hearts and souls
today protects against misfortune

if you have God in your heart
your God probably knows me
will not allow suffering
which confirms its existence

Sultana Raza

LUXEMBOURG / INDIA

Of Indian origin, Sultana Raza's poems have appeared in numerous journals, including *Columbia Journal, The New Verse News, London Grip, Classical Poetry Society, spillwords, Poetry24, Dissident Voice*, and *The Peacock Journal*. Her fiction has received an Honourable Mention in *Glimmer Train Review*, and has been published in *Coldnoon Journal, Szirine, apertura, Entropy*, and *ensemble* (in French). She has read her fiction/poems in India, Switzerland, France, Luxembourg, England, Ireland, the US, and at CoNZealand. Her SFF related work has appeared in *Entropy, Columbia Journal, Star*line, Bewildering Stories, spillwords, Unlikely Stories Mark V, The Peacock Journal*, and *impspired*. More is due to appear in Antipodean SF. Her creative non-fiction has appeared in *Literary Yard, countercurrents.org, Litro, impspired, pendemic.ie, Gnarled Oak, Kashmir Times*, and *A Beautiful Space*. Her 100+ articles (on art, theatre, film, and humanitarian issues) have appeared in English and French. An independent scholar, Sultana Raza has presented many papers related to Romanticism (Keats) and Fantasy (Tolkien) in international conferences.

FB: @sultana.raza.7
Instagram: @sultana.raza.7

WINDSWEPT VISTAS

Though Graces were hiding, and talking to both,
Infested by viruses, their minds rebelled.
Looking like tramps in sodden clothes,
They walked for miles, by poesy compelled.

Pellets of hail on bare heads fell
With ghosts and ghouls like patches grey;
Whence they came from, none could not tell.
Urged scribes to let them join their fray

Squeezed by cold, John grew sick.
Sparing William*, but not Robert**,
On him why did the Fates have to pick?
He'd soon get enough of their games covert.

Pity Scottish hills couldn't really ignite
Any poems running with deep insights.

*William Wordsworth
**Robert Burns

NOTE: July 1818. Keats is on a Scottish tour with his friend and house-mate Brown. Keats had gone there hoping to gain inspiration there, but the gruelling walking tour is taking its toll on him. Banshees, and other faerie folk are drawn to have a look at the young bard, but Keats doesn't become aware of their presence, though from time to time he gets the impression of being watched.

WINGED WISDOM

Along ferns of river, trilling flowers espied,
Crafty crows taunted, sure you'll come back?
He couldn't sort all notes, though they chirped and cried.
Owl advised him, try another tack.

Red Robin warned, don't bare your breast so.
Black bird stole away sheen of silver eyes,
Would he soon be extinct like the old dodo?
Eagle said, above all your issues you can rise.

Chatty swallows twittered, lose yourself in our chat,
Beware of quacks, cackled old duck,
Hard to forget will be wings of vicious bat,
Though doves dropped feathers for his good luck.

Kingfisher called, you're too pale.
Curlew's mournful call, chose not to heed,
Don't give up hope, intoned the quail.
Skylark's invitation? He didn't need.

Nightingale assured him, your song, I'll save,
Receded for a while, infection's shady fang.
Wood-pecker's knocks on coffin sounded grave,
Yet, unseen vibes bloomed as busy birds sang.

Silent swans on splashing streams, floated by serene,
Would his last refrain be as hauntingly keen?

Previously published on 26 December, 2020: *Winged Wisdom*/YouTube.

NOTE: birds are John Keats's friends, and try to advise/warn him as he makes his way down a river.

Francis H. Powell
ENGLAND

Francis is a poet and writer. His anthology of short stories called *Flight of Destiny* was published in 2015 by Savant Publishing, and his second book *Adventures of Death, Reincarnation and Annihilation* was published by in 2019 Beacon Publishing. At present Francis is putting together a book of short stories, poems and illustrations for the charity Marie Curie Nurses, which will be published winter 2020.
E: powellfrancisvid@gmail.com
W: www.francishpowellauthor.weebly.com
FB: @togetherbehindfourwalls

TWO CLASPING HANDS

The cement that bonds us together
with the words that soothe our souls
holding tight
in rainfall and the thunder
through all our different moods
the hand that helps
when we are feeling down
that joke we share together
fraternity can't be broken
arguments might loom
a wedge between us
but still we carry on arm in arm
we might be mountains apart
but are minds can still connect as ever
The money we give
when the needy come begging
The hand that mops up the most bitter tears
The voice that shouts out among the crowd
together we have nothing to fear
the guiding hand that shows us the way
The tight embrace when things turn ugly
A piece of advice when it is needed
a compliment when it is deserved
support when it is asked for
and protection when required
a smile of recognition
food shared when hunger calls
friendship tested over time
a friendship can be sublime

Bronwyn Vanzino
AUSTRALIA

Bron is an occasional poet, more of a novelist, more of a reader! She is currently editing her family history; telling the story of historical influences, personal and circumstantial. She is a TESOL teacher, for both migrant and academic purposes, at present more 'paused', due to Covid, than retired. She has published a couple of novels, and is included in several anthologies and publications from when she lived in Bahrain. Poetry, she believes, helps us connect with our humanity and has been much needed in the pandemic.
E: bvanzino@hotmail.com

ONLY TRAVELLING FRIENDS

You never understood
I walked on the high wire
I depended on you
To keep holding your end
Of our relationship.

Down, down I fell
As I realised
You were not there,
You were not holding on
As I transitioned to a new school.

I was a taker
In those days,
Thought people were there
For me, never read the tightrope,
Never saw the higher purpose:

That, I was the anchor man,
Not the contract walker.
Put together again,
I took shelter
In a church house.

I discovered that house had holes.
I moved to a finer house
Not realising that threatened
A new friend's church home.
Out, out in the cold I was put.

I was a taker
In those days,
Thought people were there
For me, never read the contract,
Never saw the higher purpose:

That I was a traveller,
Ever moving on,
Never remaining in the same place or with the same people,
Never at the same school, the same church,
And that even beloved family, the "permanent" ones, pass on.

Jyotirmaya Thakur
ENGLAND / INDIA

Jyotirmaya started writing when she was just seven years-old, and is now an internationally renowned poet and writer of twenty-five books She has won numerous awards, for both her literature and humanitarian efforts, and serves as Ambassador on various prestigious committees for a number of international literary and humanitarian organisations. Her work has been translated into many languages, and published in more than 500 anthologies and magazines worldwide. She exemplifies the ideal that writing is more than just words on paper; it is a means of creating positive change in the world.

E: jyotirmaya.thakur@gmail.com
FB: @jyotirmaya.thakur

FRIENDSHIP

Let's sow seeds of friendship light,
With a friendly smile, cheerful vibes,
A friendly word greeting slides,
A warm hug with healing lights.

If one person spreads smile a day,
Leading blind when crossing his way,
Holding an elder person on a busy street,
Picking up groceries for the weak.

If one person picks up abandoned,
Gave alms to beggars on roadside,
Gave poorly shelter and some food,
comfort the needy in rain or sunshine.

If friendly smiles could touch many hearts,
A penny or two to struggling musical arts,
If every person walked the extra mile,
And sowed seeds of friendship on every path.

Hussein Habasch
KURDISTAN / GERMANY

Hussein Habasch is a poet from Afrin, Kurdistan. He currently lives in Bonn, Germany. His poems have been translated into English, German, Spanish, French, Chinese, Turkish, Persian, Albanian, Uzbek, Russian, Italian, Bulgarian, Lithuanian, Hungarian, Macedonian, Serbian, Polish and Romanian, and has had his poetry published in a large number of international anthologies. His books include: *Drowning in Roses, Fugitives across Evros River, Higher than Desire and more Delicious than the Gazelle's Flank, Delusions to Salim Barakat, A Flying Angel, No pasarán* (in Spanish), *Copaci Cu Chef* (in Romanian), *Dos Árboles and Tiempos de Guerra* (in Spanish), *Fever of Quince* (in Kurdish), *Peace for Afrin, peace for Kurdistan* (in English and Spanish), *The Red Snow* (in Chinese), *Dead arguing in the corridors* (in Arabic) and *Drunken trees* (in Kurdish). He participated in many international festivals of poetry including: Colombia, Nicaragua, France, Puerto Rico, Mexico, Germany, Romania, Lithuania, Morocco, Ecuador, El Salvador, Kosovo, Macedonia, Costa Rica, Slovenia, China, Taiwan and New York City.
E: habasch70@hotmail.com
FB: @hussein.habasch

YEARNING!
To my friends who I miss so much.
Translated by Fatme Jafar

I miss you, you shadowing the eternal hardship, tenderness and letdown
I miss you just like the one who was stung at a scorching noon
I gather my demolished strengths and fly, I fly to a cloudy sky and with longing I reach you
Before I arrive, my heart reaches you on the horse of love or on the hymns of an exhausted distance
With intensive love, I step on your doorsteps, but I don't see you.

Oh! I miss you
I miss your extended tables which are like Earth's surface on the Doomsday
I play my last dice with you, I lose, and I know I will lose
It's nice, so nice to lose
So nice to lose the world with you.

I miss you
I open my memory drawers, maybe a breeze from you come to enter my eyes and the depths of my heart just like a fragrance, warmth, good tidings and the sun
Then I may be recovered by you.

Yes, I miss you
I know you have been scattered and got married to strange women
Women whose ages imitate the sunset; lusty, deviant, exhausted and divorced women.
Staring at your grey head, the wrinkles utilizing your faces and your lack of pureness, let me miss you even more and more.

I miss your lost feet in the vagrancy or in your stability as shrunken terrified cats
But you've been lost, you've even lost means of contact, you've frowned and you've ignored your devastations and letdowns.
Anyway, I miss you, your austerity, your beginnings, your rudimentary and your ancient deep cry
You've never caught your dreams which have been cracked as falling balloons
You've got lost at those unlimited crossroads since I didn't find the way to you.

Again and again I miss you
I miss your obscene insults and those vague hand signs
I miss your slurs and your shouts while you're angry
I miss your winsome deviation, your sins and your big secret pains.

I miss you
I miss your despair, your valour, the aches flowing from your eyes
and your bottles of wine
I miss your good and bad habits, but what hurts my heart is your
game with death until it wins
I miss your protuberance games and your trundled pride between
hardship jaws
I miss your noise, your stubbornness, and cock conflicts in your
minds.

I miss you
I miss your women, pardon, I mean the women of your magazines.
I miss your pleasure and your dazzling scandals
I miss your weddings, the weddings of your dreams and your sleep
with a woman a whole salacious day!

I miss you
I miss the last knife attack against your own faces and your wishes'
faces
I miss your blood circulating in your veins and revenge thoughts in
your depths
I miss you crying for each other at midnight and in the middle of your
despair you heal your wounds
I feel as if I remember you no more, but I still miss you.

I miss you
I miss you cursing all of us, your fathers, your grandfathers and your
homeland
I miss you cursing your letters which never reach but in shroud.

I always miss you
I miss your dream bikes, your barters, your elegant old clothes and
your cheapest perfumes
I miss your departing lives, your confused observations and your
despairs
Those are filled with escaping distances and the Hippies trends
emerging in your appearances.

I won't do anything except for missing you
I know you've been apart, you've quarrelled and you've longed for
each other

May I say it's not too late?
Can I say: come together hand by hand and face to face to carouse
our bottles?
Let's get drunk and play our last dice on our extended tables which
are like the
Earth's surface on the Doomsday.

But I announce the following,
Since we are filled with despair and gloom,
it's been too late to meet,
it's been too late to laugh,
it's been too late to do anything at all!

Shweta Shanker
INDIA / SWITZERLAND

Shweta was born in India, but has been living in Zurich for close to four years. An IT professional, who has held positions of software developer, program manager for executive education, and manager for a fund raising department. She is now a house manager, and finds her creative vents through writing, cooking and painting.
E: shwetashanker9@gmail.com

MY FRIEND

A finger or two, if not a hand.
A hum or two, if not a band.
A word or two, if not a line.
A spoonful or two, if not a dine.
A moment or two, if not an hour.
A candle or two, if not a star.
A smile or two, if not a laugh.
A drink or two, let it be half
my friend, don't let go, of this ebb and flow.
These are the stepping stones for my soul,
my life's story is coming together, as a whole.

Pavol Janik, PhD
SLOVAKIA

Pavol Janik PhD, is a poet, dramatist, prose writer, translator, publicist and copywriter. He has worked at the Ministry of Culture (1983-1987), and in the media and in advertising. President of the Slovak Writers' Society (2003-2007), Secretary-General of the Slovak Writers' Society (1998–2003 and 2007–2013), and Editor-in-Chief of the weekly literary publication for the Slovak Writers' Society *Literarny tyzdennik* (2010–2013). Pavol's literary works have been published not only in Slovakia, but also in Albania, Argentina, Austria, Bangladesh, Belarus, Belgium, Bosnia and Herzegovina, Bulgaria, Canada, Chile, Croatia, the Czech Republic, France, Germany, Hungary, India, Israel, Italy, Jordan, Kazakhstan, Kosovo, Kyrgyzstan, Macedonia, Mexico, Moldova, Nepal, Pakistan, Poland, the People's Republic of China, the Republic of China (Taiwan), Romania, the Russian Federation, Serbia, Singapore, South Korea, Spain, Syria, Turkey, Ukraine, United Kingdom, the United States of America, Uzbekistan, Venezuela and Vietnam.
E: mgr.art.pavol.janik.phd@gmail.com
W: www.pavoljanik.sk

THE MOMENT BEFORE TOUCH

The air grows still.
As in an illustrated weekly
I leaf through your eyes.

To hear silence
as it walks in new shoes
and lulls the buzzing bees.
Somebody furiously addresses us with wings.

It's said that you've seen
burning birds tumble from the sky!

It's just at the base of your breasts
there's something making a ceaseless hullabaloo.

TO YOU

You come from a scent.
A crumpled flower.
I inhale you tangled like smoke.

You inhabit the starry sky
and dials of digital watches.

You stupefy me dependably
and faster than light.

My head aches from you
and to this moment I mistake you for music.

ASTONISHMENT

I stretch out the water
in which you are reflected.

With a shout to stop
all possible outflows.

I address you by breath
such release of speech.
Until you are glassy with ice before me
as before a draught.

Tirelessly you quiver under the numb surface
and on the bottom for a moment gleam
so that I glimpse the day,
which will only light up in you.

William Khalipwina Mpina

MALAWI

William is a Malawian poet, fiction writer, essayist, editor, economist, business analyst and teacher, whose writing reflects on the mundane and the everyday experiences. He has works appearing in online international literary magazines such as *Kalahari Review, Literary Shanghai, Writers Space Africa, African writer, Nthanda review, Scribble Publication, Atunis Galaxy Poetry, Poetica* and *Expound Magazine*; and he is featured in over ten local and international anthologies. He is a co-editor of a poetry anthology, *Walking the Battlefield* and Tilembe Newsletter of the Malawi Union of Academic and Non-fiction Authors (MUANA).

E: williammpina3@gmail.com
FB: @Khalipwina.Mpina

FRIEND OF THE NIGHT

The night comes early in June
Cooling the warmth
Saluting the stooped stars
And my thoughts are denying me
To sleep next to you
It's been too long
And you come at night
The night whispers fear
And when you say
let's pray and sleep
And dream together
Friend, I can't do otherwise
You are already inside
But I will not share
My blanket with you

SMUDGY SUNLIGHT

it rained rough
soaked every face
nobody laughed until
higgledy-piggledy
shone smudgy sunlight
I tried to locate you
in the specks of spectators
called out your name
several times. Tired
and eyes closed
silence stood in front of me
well, you are still a friend
I just hate the direction
          you have taken.

LOVE IS NOT BEAUTY

how should I thank a dear friend
when rain clouds gathered
he came my shattered mind
to roof - and he worked so hard
while you talked and talked
I left you to talk and make
a name for yourself
that you did seductively; but
it was the depth of love
that salted the friendship
luckily, he couldn't listen to you
and guess what
yesterday he laughed
about your art of talking
that never thrilled his ear
To spoil a lasting relationship
is to chew a stone
the wind blows carrying dust
to strengthen walls of trust
built on the foundation of love
love is not beauty
love is a wave in a sobbing sea
everything fake fails to swim.

Irma Kurti
ITALY / ALBANIA

Irma is an Albanian poet, writer, lyricist, journalist, and translator, naturalized Italian. She has been writing since she was a child and has published 22 books in Albanian, 15 in Italian and four in English. She has also written about 150 lyrics for adults and children. All her books are dedicated to the memory of her beloved parents Hasan Kurti and Sherife Mezini, who supported and encouraged every step of her literary path. Kurti has won numerous literary prizes and awards in Italy and Italian Switzerland including; Universum Donna International Prize IX Edition 2013 for Literature, and the lifetime nomination of Ambassador of Peace by the University of Peace of Italian Switzerland. In 2020 she received the title of Honorary President of *WikiPoesia, the Encyclopedia of Poetry.* In 2021, she was awarded the title Liria (Freedom) by the Arbëreshë Community in Italy.
E: kurtial@yahoo.com
FB: @IrmaKurtiAutore
Instagram: @irma.kurti

MY EMPTY APARTMENT

Friends expect me to go back.
Someone else has started to dream.
In an alley of Bardhyl street,
my empty apartment awaits me.

The air is charged with memories;
missing the water, the flowers are dry.
Maybe I'll not manage to breathe;
I'll choke on the threshold.

I want to stop the flow of the crazy time;
to stay in this vacuum, never to move;
to linger here in tranquillity,
to look at the stars - pray for peace.

A METEOR

There are people you would like to encounter
on your life's path at least once again,
touch their universe with slow fingers
and share an opinion, a smile together.

You have known them only for an instant
but they remain impressed on your mind,
permeate all your thoughts like lightning
and illuminate them like a meteor does the sky.

A JEWEL

It's the time of the fading of values,
of the loss of friends one by one,
just like the trees lose their leaves
as the season of autumn arrives.

This is the time of the angry people,
no one knows: with the moon or sun,
of the ones who cannot remain silent,
of those who speak, but say nothing.

Friends are so rare. You find one,
you are suspicious, it seems unreal,
you hold and squeeze it in your palm
as a revelation, just like a rare jewel.

You keep it with anguish and interest,
careful not to drop it from your hands,
but when you slowly open your fingers,
you discover that it is no longer there.

The regret, the affliction invades you,
you realize that you've held it tightly,
you condemn yourself, it's your fault,
unintentionally you have suffocated it.

Perhaps that's why you lost it,
because you adored that jewel ...

Jojji Kaka
KENYA

Jojji is a young Kenyan freelance writer, poet and playwright from a small lakeside city called Kisumu. Jojji began writing poems at the age of 14. He specializes in poems that address social issues within the community, in an attempt to use his writing to spread positive change, and is known for his poem *Liberate*, written for a new dawn of Zimbabwe with the fall of dictator Robert Mugabe. He describes himself as a revolutionary who uses the pen as his weapon to fight social injustices.

E: georgepatrique@gmail.com
W: www.jojjikakappetrty.wordpress.com

FRIENDSHIP IS ...

Friendship is the word not spoken
The feeling not stated
Friendship is the urge to text, even when angry
Friendship is the tiny little specks of 'I care'
Hidden beneath the words of hurt.
The little pauses between words
Where you lift your head to meet their eyes
Look into them to console

Friendship is the mutual feeling of trust
Even when broken.
The minute thoughts of concern
The elemental traces of love between sentences
And the ambience of the aura around them
Friendship is the feeling of protection
The gospel of love
The taste of freedom ...

Friendship is a world, Utopia
Where joy flows from rains of silence
Where clouds are gay with every beat of a second.
Friendship is little goosebumps growing when you see them
The smile you wear when you meet them.

Friendship is the dissolving neon light in an abyss of darkness
The atom of pain when they leave
The voices of regret when you don't apologize
The weight of agony when they hurt.
Friendship is the loud voice within their silence
The garnish of worry in their words
The memory of their scent.

Words could go on
And on ...
But not consuming would they
Of what friendship spans ...

Friendship is not written
Friendship is not uttered
Its not described.
Friendship,
like a feeling -

Cocktails of between berry blossoms and writhing pain
Frown within a smile ...
Friendship,
In the moment, is LIVED!

Shikdar Mohammed Kibriah
BANGLADESH

Shikdar is a globally acclaimed poet, essayist, and short story writer, and has been writing essays on poetry, literature, philosophy, and theology over the last three decades. With an MA in Philosophy, Shikdar is a Principal of an educational institute in his village home in the Sylhet district. His works have always found renowned space in different national and international anthologies, print magazines, e-magazines, and blogs. He is involved in almost 500 literary groups, as well as different newspaper periodic issues around the world. His publications so far include fifteen books: six of poetry, another six on essay, and three short story collections. He is the Founder and President of the popular online group 'Poetry and Literature World Vision.'
E: skibriah@gmail.com

A LOVELORN CALLING

If your whole days and nights spend friendless-lonely in the midst of a crowd, then make me a call in an endearment internet - I would reach your cottage breaking knee-touched water.

If wood-packer days pass in psycho-physical agony, then send me the load of pain by Hridoypur transport - I'd unload your sorrows just my handed.

If you are unaccompanied by a constant walking, then rest a while under Hijal tree And uncover yourself by silvan fondle.

If you are sweated in a scorching summer-midday, then be seated to my veranda and unbutton your dress - southern breeze will cool your fug.

If your alluvial land is burnt in a draught, then step to the soil of a real peasant and feel how easily you will have been wet and melted with pleasant mud.

If you are burnt waterless with the fire of water, then be flashed alike Eve with the pre-historic signal of creative water.

I'll swallow your fruit of pain like a true Adam.

Kate Meyer-Currey
ENGLAND

Kate lives in Devon. A varied career in frontline settings has fuelled her interest in gritty urbanism, contrasted with a rural upbringing, and her ADHD also instils a sense of 'other' in her life and writing. Publications include: *County Lines* (Dancing Girl Press, forthcoming 2021), *Family Landscape: Colchester 1957* (Not Very Quiet. 2020), *Invocation* (Whimsical Poet, 2021), *Dulle Griet, Scold's Bridle, Recconnaissance* (*RavenCageZine*, 2021), *Fear the reaper*, (*Red Wolf Journal*, 2021), *Stream: Timberscombe* (*A River of Poems*, 2021), *Not so starry night* (*SheSpeaks*, 2021), *Dimpsey* (*Snapdragon*, 2021), *Mask* (*Disquiet Arts*, 2021), *Magnolia Stellata* (*Constellations, Literary North*, 2021), *Challenge* (*Poetry and Covid*, March 2021), *Scorpio rising* (Noctivagant Press, April, 2021), *Scrapheap Challenge* (*Handyuncappedpen*, April, 2021), *Scrubber in PPE*, (*Skirting Around*, April, 2021), *New perspective* (Planisphere HQ, April, 2021), *Hilly Fields*, (*Pure Slush, Lifespan Vol 2*, April 2021), *Kintsugi* (Aurora, Kira Kira, May 2021), *Dregs* (*Seinundwerden*, May, 2021), *Trigger* (*Collateral*, forthcoming), *Minimum credula postero* (*Ponder Savant*, May, 2021), *Palisade: Seville Oranges*, December (*Odyssey*, May, 2021), *Morning: A38, Sunflowers, Devon Autumn, Dawn Chorus, Colours of Stars* (*Bloom*, May, 2021), *Rude awakening* (*Granfalloon: A Speculative Fiction Zine*, June 2021), *Restless*, (*Open Door*, June 2021), *Purple Jellyfish Shirt* (*Mono*, June, 2021), *Re-emergence (Her Inside: Women in the Lockdown*, June, 2021). *Gloves* was also listed in the top 100 of PoetryforGood competition.
E: kateesser@live.co.uk

UNWRITTEN

For Leon

Our lives are an open book
To each other. There are some
Gaps in their shared narrative
But they're old news in our
Friendship. Anyhow, some
Of that's your story to tell.
I'm not your ghostwriter.
I cannot put words in your
Mouth. You know the skeletons
In my closet intimately. I have
Seen you close to the bone.
Our brutal honesty survived
Through dark times: drugs,
Depression, crime and debt.
I speak for both of us here.
Even the fact that we were
More than friends once has
Not changed us, in the end.
When you chose her I wished
It was me. But only sometimes
And not now. You tell me I'm
The only person who can hear
Your whole truth, down and dirty.
We both know life messes with
The plot, so no happy endings
In sight. Better just to let each
Chapter write itself, as days
Unfold into resolution: we are
Friends, still on the same page.

Rezauddin Stalin
BANGLADESH

Former Deputy Director of Nazrul Institute, and senior editor of *Magic Lonthon* - a literary organization – award-winning writer and poet Rezauddin Stalin is a well-known TV anchor and media personality, and the founder and chairman of the Performing Art Centre. He has published more than 100 books, many of which have been translated worldwide. His awards include; Darjeeling Natto Chokhro Award, India (1985), Bangla Academy (2006), Micheal Modhushudhan Dutta Award (2009), Shobho Shachi Award, West Bengal (2011), Torongo of California Award, USA (2012), Writers Club Award, California, USA (2012), Badam Cultural Award, California, USA (2012), City Ananda Alo Award (2015), West Bengal Centre Stage Barashat Award (2018), Journalist Association Award, UK (2018) and Silk Road Poet Laureate Award Xi'an China (2020).
E: rezauddinstalin@gmail.com
W: www.nazrulinstitute.gov.bd
Wikipedia: @Rezauddin_Stalin

AT THE EDGE OF EXISTENCE AND NON-EXISTENCE

My friend and I were strolling and talking
The wave of our discussion was rolling over
Breaking through the heart of the night
Flooding the street
The rejoicing radiance from the houses
On both sides
Was gleaming over
Splattering the edge of the street
Lightning emanating from our argumentative discussion
Caused jittering sparkles in the evening breeze in a magical
moonlit night.
As we were arguing over the perception of existence and
non-existence
We thought existence is a developmental process
Similar to a geometrical question
Like the evolution of a circle centring a point
And non-existence is beyond any description
like eternal silence in our heart
But none of us liked such a poetic analysis
So, we changed the subject
We said it is a beautiful night
Such a night is truly fitting for love
I said, you know once being allured by moonlight
I kissed my thirst
That magical spell still makes my eyes, lips, and heart shiver
My friend said
But when I tried to kiss the dusk
My heart trembled like that of a frightful bird
My bravery was wedged inside my throat
Hanging like sorrowful Bangla from the spike of the moon

I said, laughingly, being unmarried
Our earthly experience would be locked
Within the safety of future
my friend asked, but what is the guarantee?
The surge of our dream is bound
By the perimeter of our diminishing wealth
Our desires are blind like 'Chatak'
Being driven by our thirst
Being the citizens of the third world
Having this infertile pride
We are strolling aimlessly, without any air, food, or water.

Suddenly we realized
We came too far into a totally strange land
And the night is dark
Faint lights from few homes
Still oozing through the windows like peacock's feather
I said, for the sake of argument, we still need to say
That the sceptical society is responsible for this
My friend said that goes without saying
See every day we are being invited into the brothel of
capitalism
We praise the beauty spot on the lips of the United Nations
Within the realm of our awareness
We see that the crime against humanity
Is increasing every day.

The houses and the trees near our walkway
Were looking very lonely, very gloomy
A deadly despair
Has raised its fang towards us
I said, have you realized that unknowingly
We have entered the realm of politics
Which is crucial for our existence.

See how at this moment
Our equerries resonate with those people
Who stays up all night
Just to hear the song of 'Emu'
Who harvests to make days and nights, more momentous
Where black beauty queens
Tell their children the stories of the demonic ocean
Where diamond deer play in the land of amber soil.
See how similar are our feelings to those people
I almost screamed out of joy
Saying now is the time we find the concept of existence
But, my friend looked scared
He said, do you know
Amid overwhelming joy or sorrow, I become
speechless
And at that moment no one waits to make any decision.
Then I realized
We have to return.

Marian Dunham
ENGLAND

Marian is 66 years-old, and has been writing poetry since her school days. She loves animals and lives with a cat (the boss), an elderly collie, and her husband to whom she been married 45 years. She is also a Christian and loves nature, trees, etc., and many of her poems reflect that.
E: us2dunhams@ntlworld.com
FB: @Marians-Musings-100535154964124

MY FRIEND RACHEL

Today I lost a really good friend,
For today my good friend died.
Nothing could be done to save her,
However much was tried.
For many years we walked together,
And many miles as well.
The happy times that we both shared
Are more than I could tell.

She's always been my shadow,
Purposefully following where I led,
Never leaving nor forsaking,
Trusting as I walked ahead.

I loved her. Yes, I loved her.
She was faithful, loyal and true.
My little dog, my Rachel;
"My friend I do miss you"

Jude Brigley
WALES

Jude has been a teacher, an editor and a performance poet. She is now writing more for the page.
E: judeteach@icloud.com

THE TWO PETERS

One Summer, I joined with two Peters
to walk in the steps of Romantic poets

through the winding lanes of Somerset
and rocky outcrops of the Valley of the Rocks.

The first was older and taller, a gaunt lonely
man for whom books were solace. The other,

younger, shorter and full of the first fire
of study. We trudged to Alfoxden in the heat

of a July day, heavy with insects and unable
to magic up the spirits of the bards,

young Peter's feet aching in his new
boots. Each tried to impress me with

their readings and musings on the route.
I wanted them to get along, but at first,

they each complained of the other's
snoring, bossiness, interruptions, leaving

me perplexed until my partner interjected
at my befuddlement, saying, They are used

to impressing you and having your attention
and must now compete. Slowly, through

Lynton streets and Porlock beach, they warmed
each to the other, out-quoting in poetic

gamesmanship, until young Peter sipping
amber nectar in the Valley of the Doones

admitted that his rival was a decent chap,
but he was glad to sit out the last hurrah

of Lorna's waterfall. Instead, we played
a game of cribbage and waited for return.

I last saw the elder Peter in a bar, where,
despite the years between, we chatted

endlessly of books we read, fitting without
a seam into a friendship's sleeve. Younger

Peter always sent a card and threatened
that we would meet again. I heard his son

had William for his name. Both Peters
loved the sound of words, the fact distilled,

the camaraderie of reading and old news.
And through their walks the slow-ripening

fruit of friendship was slowly cultivated
through shared scholarly love of details.

Both died without foreshadowing
in the same year. There is a comfort

that there is a place within the brain
frozen in time when friends so privy
to your thoughts and heart still live,
a paper music score though never played.

Danielle Holian
REPUBLIC OF IRELAND

Danielle is an Irish writer and photographer, born in the West of Ireland. She studied media in college, moving on to flourish her creativity through art. She is the author of poetry books *Beautifully Chaotic*, and *The Dilemma,* and is currently working on her third book.

E: danielleholianmedia@gmail.com
W: www.danielleholian.wixsite.com/danielleholian
FB: @missdanielleholian
Instagram: @danielleholian_
Twitter: @danielleholian_

TEMPORARY

Tides turned
Leaves had fallen
And bonds grew
Until the first snowfall
With a blizzard on the way
And the pain within
I could not stay
I longed for an old love
Permanent security
Than to exchange keys
And be locked out
Of the house we built
Now lonesome
I value the survival
That I never shrunk myself
For the comfort of you
Or sacrificed my sanity
In exchange to be molded
Into all that you wanted me to be
I miss you
But the feelings come and go
Alike to seasons;
Everything is temporary.

IN THE SHADOWS

I treated you as if you had a heart like mine
As if you had a similar mindset to be kind
But the cold of the world got to you before I did
To close you off from the goodness love can bring

I am tender and I tried to let my softness comfort you
I saw your potential to embrace the security of love
Instead you banished everything
Stealing parts of me in-turn leaving me empty

I am a shadow of everything I once was;
I am still standing despite all that was set out to end me.

THE BELONGING

The roots grow deeper with stories we share
Showing compassion and hardness towards each other
That someone can love and support
Without conditions and judgement
For the tales spoken
The music listened to
The moments made together
And all the experiences shared
Sharing every detail about our lives
With long conversations
Celebrating successes
And turning up when tragedy strikes
We understand through exhaustion
When plans are cancelled
When life gets in the way
But we never give up
Being the conversation between morning tears and laughter
To the late night chatters
We are only a call away to feel we belong in this friendship.

Eliza Segiet
POLAND

Eliza graduated with a Master's Degree in Philosophy, and has completed postgraduate studies in Cultural Knowledge, Philosophy, Arts and Literature at Jagiellonian University. Her poems *Questions* and *Sea of Mists* won the *Spillwords Press* title of International Publication of the Year 2017 and 2018, and *Sea of Mists* was chosen as one of the best amidst the hundred best poems of 2018 by *International Poetry Press Publication* Canada. In *The 2019 Poet's Yearbook,* as the author of *Sea of Mists*, she was awarded with the prestigious Elite Writer's Status Award, as one of the best poets of 2019, and her poem *Order* was selected as one of the 100 best poems of 2019. Eliza was nominated for the Pushcart Prize 2019, the iWoman Global Awards 2020, and the Laureate Naji Naaman Literary Prize, 2020. Her works can be found in anthologies and literary magazines worldwide.
E: eliza.anna@op.pl

CONTOURS

Now
they don't need anything from her,
they have no reason to call
after all
she could always manage,
and they
- are fine without her.

Once again, she understood
that friendship
was an illusion.

After the years, she remembers
only the contours
of hands outstretched in need.

Once,
the sound of the phone
cut through her silence,
now
- only she remains.

Andrija Radulovic
MONTENEGRO

Andrija is a poet, essayist and editor of several literary journals. He studied History at the University of Montenegro, and graduated from the Teacher Education Faculty at the University of Novi Sad. He has received numerous literary awards, and has published the following books of poetry: *View From the Bridge, Sign in the Sand, Midnight on the Don, The Burning Rib, Word from the South* (a bilingual selection of short poems in Russian and Serbian), *Angel in the Wheat, Snowy Alphabet, The Burning Rib* (in Bulgarian and Romanian), *White Bee of Walt Whitman*, and *If I Could Cry as a Vineyard...* Radulović's poems have been published in English, Russian, Italian, Spanish, French, Greek, Bulgarian, Romanian, Hungarian, Arabic, Macedonian, Danish, Czech, Slovak, Polish, Hebrew and Ukrainian.
E: nikoladjuk@t-com.me

MY FRIEND

Translated by Nikola Djukić

My friend
Loved
Long sunsets
On the lake

My friend
Had a signature
A cardiogram
And a bamboo stick
With a red bobber

My friend
Loved
Clashing clouds
Stray dogs
Straw hats
Chimney sweeper on the roof
Storms at sea

My friend
I haven't heard from him
For some time now

A black pigeon
Landing
On my window
A black pigeon
With a letter
Still gives me hope
That he's out there
In clouds
In twilights
In storms

Alun Robert

ENGLAND

Born in Scotland of Irish lineage, Alun Robert is a Kent based prolific creator of lyrical free verse achieving success in poetry competitions across the British Isles and North America. His work has been published by UK, Irish, European, African, Indian, US and Canadian literary magazines, anthologies and webzines. He is a member of the Mid Kent Stanza, the Rye Harbour Poetry group and the Federation of Writers Scotland for whom he was a Featured Writer in 2019.
E: alanrwoods@hotmail.com

MEMORIES OF HOME

Magical moments in May
with Cantabrigiensis in bloom
gentle yellow, soft and pale
shaded under the parrotia tree

as I rest, ponder, contemplate
my heart grieving without you
when I am spirited off high
back, back to the Alborz

in sight of our Tehran
through a distant opaque
without the calm, the peace
endemic in Sissinghurst

where sweetest rose scents waft
through gardens, across beds
where I see you and sense you
in my heart. Then I cry

and clasp a prickled stem close,
ingest your fragrance
as I dream of us sharing
magical moments in May.

OUR NEW BEST FRIENDS

For our new best friends are Russian.
They live much like us.
Their families are important.
Their values are human.
They work for the big men
with whom they have no empathy.
They generate earnings
for the rich who pay little tax.

They shop in hypermarkets.
Often use convenience stores.
They eat in humble diners
or in front of televisions at home.
When there's time at the weekend,
they watch Hollywood movies.
They're passionate about sports
whatever the World series.

They receive propaganda from the media
controlled by greedy moguls.
They're told to fear us,
we brothers unarmed.
And when something is deemed corrupt,
we all get the blame.
We're all bullied by politicians
on a frolic of their own. Not ours.

Then when our elections are held
and the outcome is not per forecast,
they get the blame for involvement
while we get slated by the bitter unelected
whose values aren't humane,
whose failures are important.
Who won't live like us.
So our new best friends are Russian.

NOT ALL BAD

Sure it was me
with me tousled hair brother
what graffitied ár names
on the tall gable.
Mine was in orange.
Daryl's was the blue.
All printed in capitals
next three Viking longboats.

Dada wasn't happy -
actually furious.
Promised retribution
if we didn't whitewash it off.

Took us the weekend.
Only fell off the ladder twice.
Gardaí laughed at us.
So did ár so-called pals.
Didn't get to the bar
to watch the All-Ireland.
Didn't get to the bookies
to waste €100 on Waterford.

NOTE: The 2017 All-Ireland Senior Hurling Championship Final was the 130th event of its kind with Galway beating Waterford to win their fifth All-Ireland title.

Sandesh Ghimire
NEPAL

Sandeshis an entrepreneur, engineer, writer and poet, and has an engineering degree from Acharya Institute of Technology. As a writer he has written articles for a number of international publications including *Srujan Panicle, Kametsa magazine* (Peru) and *Homo Universalis magazine* (Greece). His recent poetry collection is titled *Peace and Harmony*. He is a life member of ARTDO International, and is currently an official convenor for the Kalika School International Advisory Board.

E: er.sandeshghimire@gmail.com
W: www.ersandeshghimire.wordpress.com
FB: @ersandeshghimire
Instagram: @sandesh_ghimire
Twitter: @_sandeshghimire

FRIENDS AND FRIENDSHIP

Piece of soul, to share
All goals and dreams together
Jokes and fun
A bond of love forever
Mountains and oceans
Beyond the cosmos
The never-ending respect
of love and regards
Similar plans, Different perception
Friend in deed and need
Daring and brave
A sacred holy bond
of friends and friendship

Cheryl-Iya Broadfoot
ENGLAND

Cheryl-Iya is an avid Soul Adventurer. Created and raised in Johannesburg, South Africa, she is now based in London. Her first adventures began in the classroom, daydreaming instead of learning, writing and poetry were always secret loves ... Chocolate and tea-lover, usually found helping women launch successful and sustainable businesses, she has been known to caress the realms of the typed-word occasionally (as a novice). She loves to follow her own soul's compass, and in doing so has found herself entertaining people with her short-stories and poems. She is self-published, twice, in self-help and a number of times in various anthologies. She is researching her third self-help book. On her journey she has met a host of writing-angels (human and celestial) all busy helping her grow her global snowball of happiness through as many means as possible, despite a number of health concerns. She carries on regardless, and enjoys it!
E: souls_compass@yahoo.com
W: www.wellbeingshowcase.com
W: www.soulscompass.net

BROKEN FAMILY, BROKEN HEART

What is a girl to do without her father there,
How will she learn that some men do care,
When will she realise love is a blessing to share,
Who will gently stroke her hair, be her partner in a pair,
The one and only who truly cares?

To build a broken heart takes a team,
A family, a village or simply to be seen,
By one upon whose strength she can lean,
Who says and does exactly what he means,
Whose trust stitches her together, seam by seam.

A broken family holds no support,
She'll have to sail rough seas to find her port,
When time's a devilish sort,
Healing is more an active sport,
Only then will life's lessons be taught:

Mending family is like mending time,
Mending hearts takes time,
Time, time, time...
More than anything this world amounts,
It's what we do with time that counts.

PAINT

If only I could paint,
I'd paint a picture for every day, every emotion:
love,
hate,
red, black, yellow, green, blue.
I'd paint dark lines,
light curves,
pretty pictures.
I'd paint a picture of you.
I'd paint a picture of me.

If only I could paint,
I'd paint a picture of our friendship:
our joy, our sorrow,
the time we spend together,
the time we spend apart,
our ups,
our downs,
the fun we have,
the problems we share.
I'd paint the best times of our lives.
I'd paint a picture of you,
I'd paint a picture of me.

If only I could paint,
I'd paint the prettiest pictures:
full of colour, full of joy,
full of black, full of pain,
full of all the things that constantly remind me
of times we've been together,
of times we've been apart,
full of things that every day remind me
of the great friend you are.
I'd paint a picture of you,
I'd paint a picture of me:
I'd paint a picture of our friendship.

John Notley
THAILAND / ENGLAND

John was a travel agent for 40 years but, now retired, spends much of his time in Thailand where he attempts to write short stories and the occasional poem. Over the years he has had a number of these published in a variety of publications. He prefers to write rhyming poetry which is now considered old style. Which prompts the question; how many non-rhyming poems will be remembered and recited in years to come?
E: john.notley@gmail.com

MY FRIEND THE CAT

My feline friend sits patiently
fixing me with sphinx-like stare
when I arise to rake the ashes
takes his place with arrant pride
leaps upon my favourite chair.

As he surveys his kingdom,
languishing with grace
what fiendish plans are laid
what cat-like thoughts are present
behind that enigmatic face?

Why does this haughty creature
arouse such fear and awe
at times so soft and cuddly
whose gentle purring masks
the claw within a velvet paw.

Worshipped by the Pharaohs
sired of ancient blood
how can a simple moggie,
a scruffy alley cat
be worthy of my love?

Mahrukh Asmat
PAKISTAN

Mahrukh is a 20 year-old writer and poet, and manages a WordPress website. She always hopes to make her writings as genuine as possible; to let people feel what she feels when she's writing. Most of her writing focusses on human feelings and experiences, and the transitioning of different phases of life. She has also published some of her work with online magazines, and is aiming for a career in freelancing.

E: manocrafts0248@gmail.com
W: www.armadaliterature.blog
Instagram: @armada.blogger

FRIENDS

Paint my eyes, weave my mind,
So a friend in you, my eyes find.
I find foes in every stranger.
I find lies, deceit and danger.

Float my thoughts on a wispy cloud,
Lull my demons singing loud.
Lit in flames, my mind is hell.
My peace, my trust, everything's a shell.

O Friendship, where art thou?
My life is empty, tell me how
I can trust again and find a friend,
And my sorrows, to another, lend.

Yi Jung Chen
TAIWAN

Yi Jung (Jolene) writes poems in English, Chinese and Taiwanese. Besides teaching students of learning difficulties at Dounan Elementary School in Taiwan, she also earned her doctoral degree from Graduate Institute of Education of National Chung Cheng University in 2015. In her spare time, Jolene also works with other teachers for the completion of illustrated picture books in Chinese, English and Japanese language.
E: jolenechen@tnps.ylc.edu.tw
Instagram: @ymay86
Twitter:@YiJungChen3

THE COSMOPOLITAN LADIES

Under the hazel tree,
drinking the cosmopolitan cocktail with you,
whatever the ages and experiences are,
the image of petrel always remains fresh in our hearts.

Watching the ebbs and flow of the tide,
running barefoot on the sand,
laughing all the way till
the sunset and the moonlight call us lunatic.
The breeze gently hit our faces,
awakening my torpid senses,
the moment slipped away, as if
our footprints were washed away,
by surging waves.

A photo frame did not limit our vision,
making a toast to each other,
we prayed for everything unchanged
when we return from our voyage someday,
like a plover,
start-and-stop for the happiness,
rises over the horizon of ocean.

Zorica Bajin Djukanovic
SERBIA

Zorica graduated from the Faculty of Philology of Belgrade University, the Department of Yugoslav Literature. She writes poetry, prose and literature for the young, and has published a total of seventeen books including the collections of poetry *Blood Clot* (1994) and *Lining* (1999), the short story collections *Hotel Philosopher* (2003) and *Said King Of Sunshades* (2009) and the following collections of poetry for young people: *Wizard* (1999), *Tiny Box For A Firefly* (2010), *Summer Day* (2014) and *Brief Love Poems* (2017). Her poetry and prose have been translated into Russian, English, Dutch, Rumanian, Ruthenian and Macedonian, and her work has been featured in 60 anthologies, chrestomathies, textbooks and readers. She lives and works in Belgrade, Serbia, as a freelance artist.
E: poemleto@gmail.com

ENAMEL

For Milutin Petrović

Translated from the Serbian original by Novica Petrović.

During bouts of fever
Under my pillow I put Relaxan
His book
Hoping it might take my head
To my cloud
But from the slippery covers I slide straight
Through the whirlpool of the title
Onto a page half unstitched
From browsing
Into a poem with a tiny light
And a small mirror
Wherein I never manage
To recognise my face
And due to teeth chattering
Remove a little enamel from the front ones
So the book is increasingly more mine
And increasingly less his
For it is padded with my mother-of-pearl

And so I slide down the pages
And fall through the membranes of verses
Who else would make
Artificial cumulus clouds for me
To keep me
Above the poetry of dreams

LEAFING
For Sylvia Plath
Translated from the Serbian original by Novica Petrović.

I am Sylvia's friend
Sylvia likes perfect things
For a perfect smile
She would remain on the edge of its shadow
Her men are perfect too
I would not dare dream of them
No one has seen us together
That is the attraction of our friendship
We like shady bowers
And nocturnal tea with a couple of drops of summer

Silvia is a being full of ink
And her man has the task
Of being her inkwell and her lover
I watch him as he stumbles
Absorbing her running wishes
And avoid looking him in the eyes
Sylvia sends her children
Into the unknown without much thought
I watch her perfect children
Gathering seashells on the shore
And think how good it is
That they don't take after her

Through a fine numbness Sylvia always feels the pain
Of bruises serving as proof that she was there
When the hood
Of unpurified time is lowered
It sucks in
The manifold forms of fear
All those who have tried it
Have become useless witnesses
That is why Sylvia always softens a description of coming down
In order to convince us
That it is not so terrible
That is Sylvia's greatest gift

Sylvia likes to hide
She sometimes crawls into the darkness of a trunk
For transoceanic voyages

Other times she curls up cat-like
In the gas oven holding her breath
When I find her
It is not in another room
Or in another corner of our room
But in her sharpened gaze
Lowered to the bottom

Onoruoiza Mark Onuchi
NIGERIA

Onoruoiza Mark Onuchi is a creative wingman, wordsmith and poet, with poetic offerings across a wide array of anthologies. He wrote the foreword to the highly acclaimed collection of poems titled *Oracle* by Dayo Ibitayo Phillips. He has his poetic offerings in *Crossroads* (an anthology of poems in honour of Christopher Okigbo: 1932–1967, edited by Patrick T. Oguejiofor and Kalu Uduma), *Echoes and Voices from the Midland*, an anthology of poems (Unilorin Press) edited by Isiaka Aliagan, and *The President and other poems* edited by Adjekpagbon Blessed Mudiaga (Bulkybon books). He has his elegies in *Wreaths for a Wayfarer*(Daraja Press) - an anthology of poems in Honour of Pius Adesanmi, edited by Nduka Otiono & Uchechukwu Umezurike. *The 2020 Poetry Marathon Anthology* edited by Shloka Shankar has his contribution too. He's also been featured in the *Guardian* and *Thisday* newspapers in Nigeria.

E: markonuchi@gmail.com
FB: @onuchi.mark
Instagram: @markpoet
Twitter: @markpoet

MY LOVESOME JEWEL

For my heartthrob, Adetutu.

My love for you
is like an endless ocean
boundless - beyond limit.
My love for you
is like the blazing sun
fiery – passionate to no end.
My love for you is like the diamond
priceless – radiant sparkle
with unalloyed polish.
My love for you is like unblemished gold
precious – superlatively irreplaceable.
My love for you
is like the moon
luminescent - burnished
with an ageless glow.
My love for you
is like the sky
celestial - above the mortal reach
of the earthy!
Ours is an Eden of never ending bliss
flavoured with the paradise of idyllic infinity.
You are indeed the one
to whom my heart beats,
my cherished jewel
to whom my heart yearns;
my ornate gem
to whom my heart desires …
Your unsullied warmth,
your untarnished grace
graphically encapsulates
the luscious charm of my genial cherub!
May you continue to outshine
the stars with your seraphic sparkle!

BROTHERHOOD

Friendship is a fusion -
an eclectic mix of brotherhood
mutual affection and selfless solidarity!
We are wired
with the mesh of communal steel
the loyalty of bonds that binds
two independent fellows
to forge the path of light
beaming through novel tunnels
for collective triumph ...
The wakeful fire of unending flight -
You, I
We conquer them
A win,
we all deserve –
this is a toast to friendship!

AMBITION

I nursed a vision
of you
at dawn
reinforced at noon
until I met you.
The intersection
struck a tie -
a fusion
built to outlast
the test of fire
and the passage of time –
eternal!
Your presence
transformed my mission
with a passionate evolution.
it sparked a fresh fire
from within.
Bursting barriers
terminating strongholds
that once blurred my vision.
Now I see
Beyond the horizons
of visualisation
sharper than the eagle's
I am here ...
To take on the world
slouching on flippant mode
to rattle the norms
rewrite the rules
with an empowered might.
Thanks to you!

Margaret Macdonald
SCOTLAND

Margaret was born in Colombo, Sri Lanka, and moved to London in 1959. Since 1985, she has lived in rural Aberdeenshire, Scotland, where she studied, raised her children and worked. Margaret is a qualified social worker, mediator, and trainer, and a member of Huntly Writers. During the 2020 lockdowns, Margaret began work on a children's book about a naval hero cat named Simon who was awarded the Dickin Medal for bravery - the animal equivalent of the Victoria Cross. Margaret discovered Simon's story five years earlier, through her mother-in-law Mary, and was inspired to write a rhyming tale for children about this extraordinary cat. *The Ballad of Able Seacat Simon of HMS Amethyst* is her first children's book independently published in November 2020.
E: Margaret.macdonald2020@outlook.com
W: www.margaretmacdonaldauthor.com
Twitter: @AbleSeacatSimon

KWOK YI

Hey!
What kind of person is she?
Who bonds like an albatross with the strength of a tree.
Whose apparel mimics bright jungle fowl.
Whose equable spirit makes clenched fists uncurl.

Magnanimous AND canny,
She spreads little afar.
Her pithy perspective vivifies any hour.
Eschewing what's wrong,
August she has stood.
A counterpoise to evil,
An acme of good.

In stature exiguous
But a fugleman is she.
Leading a march to play, fun, and glee.
Unclassifiable, she still has a name.
Called Renny, by many.
By me, A Dear Friend.

AUTHOR'S NOTE: This poem is about my friend from Hong Kong. Her Chinese name is Kwok Yi. In Scotland, she is called Renny. It was written for her 60th birthday in May 2021.

Srimayee Gangopadhyay
INDIA

Srimayee is a 22 year-old poet from West Bengal, currently pursuing Masters in English Literature. For Srimayee, poetry is a means of introspection, a dive into nostalgia and connecting with self. She started writing poems at the age of 11, while searching for enigma in the ordinary and as a mechanism to uncover her introverted self. She critique films on various e-platforms, and interpret works of eminent poets/writers. Her poetic inspirations include Leonard Cohen, Emily Dickinson, Sylvia Plath, Keats, Wordsworth, among others.
E: srimayee98@gmail.com
FB: @srimayee.ganguly.3

TWO RED KAPOKS

The wind heaved a sigh as heavy as mine,
Shoved me strong, swayed my way
Into the fallen inflamed fronds-
With a familiar stranger among them.
That marked the day I saw another self -
Who also loved to taint his pages in petals of wine;
He held his red kapok, in bold bloom near my ear;
A curl of my lips and I shook the pollens off my hair.
Unmoved in defiance, overruled by passion, oh!
But how they mistook two souls for one -
Just like you couldn't distinguish your red silk cotton
From the one pinned in my tome.
The seas made sure we had it our way
Waves of burgundy under an electric sky,
Perhaps they knew, only too well,
How breath may falter though souls unite.
The earth made you hers; maybe you were never mine;
Maybe the foams of our bottled love did us beguile ...
Where kapoks red, unrivalled in pairs, may come undone,
I'll still not get over how they mistook two souls for one.

Nupur Shah

INDIA

Nupur recently graduated from the University of Mumbai with a B.A. in English. *"We do language. That may be the measure of our lives."* This quote by Toni Morrison is what she wishes her poetry will come to swear by.

E: shahnupur101@gmail.com

FOR AN INTIMATE STRANGER

Words break through
The uncharted map
Of what was once life
But is now mundanely called
Childhood, or, a sane happiness

We were friends, some said
Others bestowed the compliment
Companions for life
But we alone knew (what we knew)
That words would not suffice
To claim who we were

What are we?
Human beings or beasts being devoured by time?

Let us stray from answering this one
As we must from countless others
That raise terror like mountains
Running wild like rivers
Swamping the unploughed land
Some call memory; some, regret

Once upon a time when we hadn't lost our minds
We were happy
Is that what they call being
Together, holding each other

For if the world got this right
Then neither I nor you
Ever knew it too well

Aided by our ignorance
You exited its customs, its habits
In whose narrow width
Both I and you
Friends once, are now silent
Except when the storm of defeat
Of naive promises made in their glory
Rages like a fire in the forest of life
And from the tempest trampling my soul

One question arise:

Where do friends go when the ship as sailed to other, foreign shores?

TRIUMPHANT

Death was too proud
But we had our graces
Yours, the courage of hope
Mine, the hope of courage

Wrecked on the same shore
We were rummaging on opposite ends
You for the morphine and the wigs
I for my Cloak of Invisibility

All the time we fought the colossus
In hospital rooms and on ambulance rides
I was filing with the rancour of being
The weaker, meeker, seeker one

For weren't you the one who found
Without having to look anywhere
For those reservoirs of strength
That made you ever-triumphant?

They broke the day you died
Hanging by a thread you left with me
Cling to this, the last bit of my life
If you survive, it would be my triumph

And so I do, at least until
This business of eulogizing finishes
After this, I will drift away
From the tip of needles and the blaze of lights

After you all will be hard to hold
Least of all, *the last bit of my life*
Stringing a lonely song in my heart
That now beats tirelessly

But I know this
That one day, some day, it must tire
Must cease to repeat endlessly
The corrupting triumph of my life
In the war between my body and her spirit

Sunitha Srinivas C
INDIA

Sunita works as Associate professor in a government college in Keral. She as published books and poems with leading international publishers both within and outside her country
E: sunita.srinivas@gmail.com
FB: @suni.srini
Instagram: @sunitha_srinivas_c

YET, HOPE KEEPS LIFE

A hand that held me tight
Taken away
Holds me still

Taught me not to falter, to wane nor wither
Held me firm on paths mine own
Taught of love wasted
Of a life squandered in giving

Eyes that searched, waited and hoped
Shoulders that held me close and high
Withered and skeletal became on my cheeks

A heart heavy with wishes
Easy to hurt and break
Lifeless, lay on the floor
Reluctant to forgo my love
Or leave me amidst a whirlpool life

Hope hurts
For it's broken
Like a promise

Veda Varma
KINGDOM OF BAHRAIN / INDIA

Veda is an Indian teenager living in the Kingdom of Bahrain. She is a poetry, guitar and drama enthusiast. Her talent and love for poetry came as a complete surprise when a school assignment pushed her to give poems a try. Writing has now become one of her greatest passions, and writes about topics that leave the reader puzzled and questioning themselves.
Instagram: @_houseofpoetry

THANK YOU AND I APOLOGIZE

There are times,
We feel defeated.
There are times,
We feel broken.
There are times,
We feel worthless.

The dismal times we go through,
Not many have a breakthrough.
This perpetual void of darkness,
Leaves us portrayed as 'heartless,'
Even though, there is too much hurt, too much pain,
Too much to recover from,
We forget, there is much more to come.

Believe me, I have been shattered too,
Caught in the rip tide of my being.
I have felt drowned,
With no hope of being found.

Yet, someone came and pulled me out,
Someone who never had a doubt.
Someone who believed I was worth saving,
Someone who kept praising, even when I was failing.

Elna, I thank you for your existence.
Thank you, for meeting me 11 years ago,
Thank you, for helping me grow,
Thank you, for shielding me from anything the world threw.
Thank you, for noticing my beauty,
A beauty, I never let myself feel,
Thank you, for helping me heal.

You don't know who much you're worth,
You don't know how many you've helped since your birth,
You don't know how many smiles you are the cause of,
You don't know how many out there are grateful for your love.

I would like to end this poem with an apology,
I apologize for not helping you enough,
I apologize if I neglected you during the rough and tough,
I apologize if you felt unheard,

I apologize for every word,
That ever hurt you.

I hope you feel loved as you love.
I hope for an eternity of smiles for you,
You have helped so many, you have no clue.
Keep changing for the better,
As change is inevitable.
However, never lose yourself,
You're a miracle in itself.

Rema Tabangcura
PHILIPPINES / SINGAPORE

Rema is a domestic helper in Singapore and started writing poetry during the Covid pandemic. One of her poems titled *The Beauty Within* was featured in The Substation theatre play called *allieNation* in November, 2020. She is also a volunteer team leader at a non-profit organisation called Uplifters; providing online education courses about Money Management and Personal growth for migrant domestic workers around the world.
E: rematabangcura@gmail.com

BESTFRIEND

You are the person,
Whom I have strong connection.
Someone I know,
From head to toe.
Standby me consistently,
Both when I'm present
And when I'm not around.

Aren't phony,
when saw the negative side of me.
Never leave me,
no matter how contagious I am.
You show me who you really are,
Authentic as a precious gem.

You can see tears,
pouring inside me.
While others believe,
the smile I'm faking.
You were a great listener,
and never been a judgemental.

You have a magic effect,
that makes me like you in an instant.
You are more fun,
than anyone I know.
And that makes our bond,
stick like a glue.

Whenever I have a tiff with my family,
you always find a way to help me.
Staying afar with each other is not a hindrance,
Feels like you are near, never apart.

Your outlook in life is amazing,
And I thank the Almighty,
for giving me such a great blessing.
To you my Friend,
I will cherish our bond,
Until beyond.

Kristine Ventura
MALAYSIA / PHILIPPINES

Kristine is a mother of two, born in the Philippines but currently working in Selangor, Malaysia for five years. She started embracing poetry recently, and has been guided by some of her virtual friends, and now poetry has become a part of her daily life.
E: venturakristine32@gmail.com

HIDDEN LOVE

Wearing a mask of sorrow,
I walk with my shadow.
With a weakened body,
I continued my journey.
Not knowing where to go,
I kept on going through.

You found me helpless,
In the middle of darkness.
You held my hand slowly,
You lift me up gently.
Out of the blue I cried,
Those pains can't no longer hide.

You lend your ears,
You wipe away my tears.
You said "trust me my dear"
Yet I refused because of fear.

You took me to an open door,
And guided me as we explore.
You let me in into an open hall,
Where in my face painted on the wall.

Now I know why you always care,
Now I know why you're always there.
You're my soulmate, sent from above.
Thank you for the hidden love.

Aminath Neena
MALDIVES

Aminath has an MA TESOL from the University of Nottingham, and is an English lecturer. An avid lover of words, poetry is a hobby closest to her heart. Her poems usually revolve around themes such as love, relationships, spirituality, society, and global issues. According to her, poetry is the gateway to spirituality because it resonates with purity like no other. She recalls her first major achievement as having her poem *Dystopia* featured in *Words and Music*, a programme on BBC Radio. Her poems are published or are forthcoming in a range of international platforms like the *Trouvaille Review, Spill Words, Muddy River Poetry Review, Inspired* magazine, *Continue the voice* magazine and *Borderless Journal*. Her poems have also been published in a number of anthologies including *Eccentric Orbits* by Dimensionfold publishing and *Poetica 2* of Clarendon House publications.
E: aminathneenahanyf@gmail.com
FB: @aminath.neena

GOLDEN DREAMS
Dedicated to my best friend of 30 years.

Do you not remember the times we had wings to fly as the
dragonflies
Soaring higher and higher
whimsical and carefree as ever
Oh! how we danced with the breeze
You and me, as shadows of each other

Do you not remember the times we used to gaze at the shooting
stars
A thirst for simple desires
a hunger for forbidden tastes one after the other
Dreaming of castles and fairies
and making wishes for each other

Do you not remember the times we bloomed into scented flowers
often sharing each other's petals
so that we had combinations of feather
of colours of the spring blossoms
and brought out the best in one another

Do you not remember the times we tasted the sugar cane in the
fields
Trespassing in alien territory
Always victorious with no regrets whatsoever
Forever dodging the consequences
Being alibis to save each other

Do you not remember the times we tied the world with the ribbon of
our ponytails
you and me sharing a laugh or two
saving the golden titbits for times that matter
giggling and running on bare feet
being the racing wind of each other

Do you not remember the times of sadness and grief
How you held me close to you
as we let down our waterfalls together
how I wiped your tears and held your hand
we were strong, being pillars for each other

Inseparable like the skin on flesh we were! Don't you remember?

Though, times may have changed and you live in a dark abyss now
I still pray with all my heart that someday the wall will shatter
For this, I must say that the love I have for you is guaranteed
to remain true so long as the golden sun smiled, over the earth
mother

THE SILVER BUTTERFLY

Do you still remember or think about
That silver butterfly with wings of cheese blue
With a stick full of breadfruit sap, as glue
The one, in spring you chased all around?

I can still recall your surprise
When I had gained its trust
And wiping my hands of its powdery dust
I gave it to you gently as a prize

Though I never told you how I had it
so calm and composed within my fist,
I will do so as this year's 'New Year gift'
When we celebrate of love- three decades of it

Well dear, it so happened in a trot
That while I sat day dreaming
Under the guava tree counting
the petals of daisies, for love and love not

That silvery angel came and sat on my ringlets
Right down my cheek it was moving
straight into my heart it was aiming
For a while it tickled as I ignored the bets

When it sat on my ring finger
I saw its sweetness clearly
And then I knew instantly
Without a single streak of waver

Why you yearned for it so much
So, without so much of a hesitation
As it fluttered its wings in frustration
And - though it was as sweet as blueberry fudge

I caught it in my hand again
and simply gave it to you so
I only had a little of its dust and no more
preferring my loss for your gain

But then I still wonder today, ma cherie
Whether, then I did the right thing

as it seems that it was only a passing fling
For you have found your "mon cheri"

And I do wonder where that butterfly is now
Perhaps roaming just like me- high up above?

Kate Young
ENGLAND

Kate is semi-retired and lives in Kent. She is a teacher and has been passionate about poetry since childhood. With a love of Art, Kate writes a lot of Ekphrastic poetry and enjoys visiting galleries for inspiration. She also loves reading, dancing, painting, and playing the guitar and ukulele, and belongs to three poetry groups which have helped and supported her in recent years. Her poems have appeared in *Ninemuses, Ekphrastic Review, Nitrogen House, The Poetry Village, Words for the Wild, Poetry on the Lake, Alchemy Spoon* and two Scottish Writers Centre chapbooks. Her work has also featured in the anthologies *Places of Poetry* and *Write Out Loud*. Her pamphlet *A Spark in the Darkness* won The Baker's Dozen competition with Hedgehog Press, and is due to be published. Her poem *The Last Stars* was shortlisted in The Poetry on the Lake Competition 2021.
E: kateyoung12@hotmail.co.uk
Twitter: @Kateyoung12poet.

FOR PIM
Died July, 2020.

My childhood was a daisy chain,
beautifully flawed, fragile.
One slip of stem, the link would break
but you were always there,
stationed next door
anxious eyes a fret through glass.

I would appear at the gate
knees raw from scraped bark
or eyes sore from beach-salt.
I still feel the scoop of you,
hands doused in Dettol
adept in the art of healing.

You have been a constant.
I cannot imagine a dawn
without your freckled smile
but 2020 has claimed you
stolen our right to mourn.
Pockets of black
scatter like ants

long to touch   hug   console.
I sense your presence,
imagine your laugh
tearing through masks,
the absurdity of it.
You connect me to this earth,
I am threaded in memory.

Aleksandra Vujisić
MONTENEGRO

Aleksandra is a professor of English language and literature, and a passionate writer of prose and poetry. She has participated in poetry festivals across Europe, and her works have won prizes and acknowledgements both in Montenegro and worldwide. Aleksandra writes in her native language and English, and her stories and poetry have been published several times and translated into Italian and Spanish. In 2017 she started a literary project in order to promote the importance of reading for children, and starting from May 2021 she is a member of the Association of Montenegrin authors for children.
E: Aleksandra.vujisic@gmail.com

THE END, MY FRIEND

Oh, my dear friend!
Let me hold your dreams while you shake off
the golden dust from your skirt,
and let me release my hopes
that there is nothing left for you to get hurt.

Let me open those curtains that hide the light
from your memories,
let me share with you all the magical herbs,
let my words be your remedies.

Let me hold your pain while you slowly
walk done the path of never found peace,
and let me protect your eyes, wings of a
powerful bird that needs to be released.

Let me hold your fear like a flower
in my hand,
let me share the loss, then the power
of coming to an end.

ESCAPE

Let's run together and let's try to make
up for the lost days -
Let's nor wait for plans to make big voyages,
let's escape from reality,
empty words and promises.

Don't allow any fairy tales to be made
on what is left behind our friendship,
let all the winds give us new power
without fears - let's board this ship.

Let's run there where time is important
only when happiness is counted, day and night,
where mountains echo honestly and strongly
and darkness is afraid of the light.

Let's run together! Pack everything you
are good at in the luggage,
and let's forgive the mistakes without pretending,
life can't hide from those like us,
don't stop dreaming, searching, understanding.

Zana Coven
ITALY / SPAIN

Zana was born in Sarajevo, Bosnia Herzegovina and, as a child, studied English language and literature. After graduation she moved to Belgrade to study Spanish and Italian, and then to Italy for further studies. She worked as a translator, teacher, coordinator and supervised of cultural projects for many years, and was one of co-founder of jazz experiment group *Mode*, playing saxophone and clarinet. She is also an artist, and has had several exhibitions in Italy and Spain, as well as in 2017 in Široki Brijeg, Bosnia Herzegovina, which she dedicated to her parents. Zana writes poetry, haiku, short stories and travel books in English, Spanish, Italian and Croatian. Her four books of poetry are; *Lo dico alla luna*, (in Italian), *Entre sol y sombra* (in Spanish), and *Zaboravljena u stihu* (*Forgotten in a Verse*) and J*edna Ljubav* (*One love*) (in Croatian). Her poetry and short stories have also been published in a number of books, magazines, almanacs and blogs worldwide including in Portugal, Spain, Mexico and Japan, and her haiku has been published in *Asahi International* magazine, *Asahi haikust* and *Akita Internazionale haiku*. Zana has also won a number of international prizes including being profiled in the book *26 Women of Essence* published in Sidney, Australia, and the forthcoming *25 Women of Virtue* in India. She works and lives between Milano and Barcelona.
E: zana.coven61@gmail.com

FRIENDSHIP

Two heads that
Trust each other
Four eyes that
Look in the
Same direction
Open hearts
For secrets
Open hands
To help
Smiles
To cherish
Company
To share
Two worlds that
Support
Each other
Universe at
Glance

Big burdens
To bear
Sincere loyalty
To swear
So many stories
To share
Too many ideas
To dare
The same path
To walk
So many troubles
To talk
Coffee or tea
To drink
The same thoughts
To think
Never to feel
Alone
Hours and hours on
Phone
So strong is this
Bond
When that one you
Found

David Hollywood
REPUBLIC OF IRELAND

David has lived and worked around the world. While in Bahrain he helped form The Bahrain Writers' Circle, and then The Second Circle poetry group in readiness for what annually became The Colours of Life Poetry Festival, one of the biggest poetry events in the region. David also contributed to the bestselling *My Beautiful Bahrain, More of My Beautiful Bahrain* and *Poetic Bahrain*, and was *Bahrain Confidential*'s in-house poet, and literary critic for T*he Taj Mahal Review*. He has contributed to a further fifteen volumes of literary and poetry editions, as well as various international magazines. David is also the author of *Waiting Spaces*, an eclectic collection of some of his poems, and his forthcoming I*ntuitions Instincts* is due to be launched in 2021.

E: davidhollywood23@hotmail.com

MELANCHOLY, LOVE & TRUST

What has happened to worn chairs and wooden tables;
With a carafe of wine and old oranges?
In a garden together with friends,
Who greet you with their welcome,
And support of each other.

It belongs to some other time!

Imagine a walk through a thin wood,
To the edge of a rise!
To discover the finest of views in the morning,
Finding dew in the middle of your thoughts,
And the sun has already started to warm.

At the end I should love the world to be elegant.

To know my company was anticipated!
Enough to say, "good day."
Fine manners and virtued behaviour,
With the best of company,
And only that which is true and noble.

And nothing of these times.

Mark Andrew Heathcote

ENGLAND

Mark is from Manchester. His poetry has been published in many journals, magazines and anthologies worldwide, and is the author of *In Perpetuity* and *Back on Earth,* two books of poems published by a CTU publishing group - Creative Talents Unleashed. Mark is an adult learning difficulties support worker, who began writing poetry at an early age at school.
E: mrkheathcote@yahoo.co.uk

HEREAFTER ...

Life should close like a book of poems
with no real end in sight!
Just a half-remembered mystery,
that once was a friend when life did smite.

Life should close like a book of poems
owing, nothing to it, chum!
Other than a modicum of laughter ...
or even a word to the wise in the hereafter.

Sam Eastwood
NEW ZEALAND

Sam lives in Tauranga, a city in the North Island. He began writing twenty years ago when he started a SF novel - a love story with poetry. It was then that his passion for poetry began. He wrote several poems for the book, and for friends, which later became a trilogy of love poems, and is now an internationally published author. He writes love poems, spiritual poems, short stories, and thoughts about life, and his work has been published in various magazines and literary blogs, and translated into a number of languages.

E: sam@poems-by-sam.com
W: www.poems-by-sam.com

GOOD FRIENDS

Finding One?
You look
"Where are they?" you ask.
"Well," I say,
"That falls into the saying,
I'd have to Love you if I told you."
"?." She thinks.
I say, "We can all desire to be good friends."

Good friends,
Those that share with understanding,
who we each are, in a trustful relationship
Without wishing to change this aspect
This is a simple choice
Which will change your life,
And those we engage with through our years
With soulfulness, be good friends.
Living peacefully, and in kindness.

How simple is that?
when by chance this becomes
Anything more, we are Free to travel
deeper into each other's lives,
with wisdom, and faithfulness
be illuminated with the richness
of God's creation.

A MUSE

Beautiful and magically imagined
An Inspired women, of grace and presence
Sensual, exotic and intuitively aware
Holding my heart with love
In love and
My Muse.

How long, how far, was my search?
Love was around, as I loitered against
The invisible post of procrastination
Where time has hold, and to mould
Deeper emotions, colourful bubbles
Bursting into illuminating fragrances

I love, with my Souls commitment
What was or is meant to be
May not be free
To Love
And thus to be trapped, soundless
Dreams with dark corners

Love's partner, Faithfulness and Trust
Follow as you wander experiencing
The wonders along your path
My heart is filled with gratitude
Enlightenment and Understanding
Why Love has brought me here, to you.

A POEM
For Ana

I never learnt to play the piano
Yet my fingers, on porcelain dance
A soft melody, within my heart
to bring such feelings and emotions
I desire you to hear from my Soul

With love

Let not us be alone, and agree
Our lives were meant to be
Those notes upon the score
Freed from the page, no longer
Surrounded in silence, and declare...

With wisdom and understanding
I love you being a part of my life
And along the paths we willingly
Chose to wonder, in grace and peace
We have discovered each other

Sam

Xanthi Hondrou-Hill
GREECE

Xanthi studied German Literature and Linguistics at the University of Stuttgart, Journalism at the University of Hohenheim, and Public Relations Management at Klett-WBS in Stuttgart. She has lived in Greece, Germany, Holland and Great Britain, speaks several languages, and has worked as a multi-lingual teacher, journalist, public relations manager and poet, and is currently working as public relations consultant for the European Art Platform *Apeironart*. Xanthi has organised in the past years many poetry events in cooperation with the local municipality and the archaeological secretary of the Prefecture of Imathias, and in Germany she worked as Public Relations Manager for the Greek General Consulate in Stuttgart, designing, organising and executing multi-level campaign to improve Greek awareness in Germany. Her poems have been published in the *University Newspaper of Stuttgart* and other well-known publications including the *Stuttgarter Zeitung*. Additionally she has participated in numerous anthologies in cooperation with the Greek Society of Writers in Germany, and in *Almanac,* the annual anthology of the House of Writers in Stuttgart. In Greece she runs a cultural Facebook page dedicated to poetry and arts, and organises events including 'Poetry on Rails.'
E: xanthihondrouhill@gmail.com

MEDITERRANEAN WAVES ...

Three blue poets
fill our life
one singing the blue from the sky
the other the waves of the sea
and the third whispers the wisdom of the wind

No matter to which shores the poem takes us
with which clouds we want to travel
with the wave of a blue scarf
or the white sail of a boat
the wing of a plane
there is always the wisdom of the wind to carry us

To reach the shores of dreams
with flowers, pebbles and sea shells as treasures.
The nights were we talked at blue tables with friends
or on the phone miles away, listening to the tide
The fun we shared travelling in a rental car without lights
on an island looking to avoid a monastery
and ending up spending the day there in the arms of a Saint
bringing with us healing oils and sacred water

The paintings we discovered in the small museum, in our faces
and on the street corners looking down to the sea
feeding a foreign hungry artist at the little coffee shop by the seaside
We didn't exchange letters and alphabets like our ancestors
didn't care if the numbers were Arabic or Greek
didn't even try to find common ground
because three blue poets, a painter and a musician
filled our life
with the waves of the Mediterranean ...

TIE
For Dimitris Parolas, Conductor of the Naoussa Conservatory,
Naoussa, 2019.

Planted
on the horizon
hopes and dreams
a poem
in first inversion
And hung my heart
on the key of the non-existent scale

on the pentagram of the sky
birds will write
the future
of our lasting connection

Achingliu Kamei
INDIA

Dr Kamei is a poet, a short story writer and an ultra-marathon runner. Her poetry has been published in several journals and in anthologies from India, USA, Singapore and Australia including *Setu International Journal, Borderless, Poetry Pea Journal of Haiku and Senryu* and *Melbourne Culture Corner*. She finds it most therapeutic to write Haiku verses. She is currently living in Delhi, with her husband, two daughters and Haru the cat.
E: achingliuk@gmail.com

SHE IS THE WATER FILLING YOUR EMPTINESS

When she goes silent, you listened to her soul
In the silence of the lull, your soul listened to her heart
You come to her with your thirst and hunger
You seek her for peace and tranquillity
Her words are the seeds sown in your field
You reap with gratitude the fruits.

The warmth of her love; the comfort at her fireside
Her best food you eat; her garden for the hungry
She is the water filling your emptiness,
Deepening your friendship, and love
Friendship that last this life and beyond.

No need to second guess her deeds or read between lines
She is the ebb of your tide, she twinkles and glows
She is the angel you can see, guiding you when you get lost
She is the river you see from the peak, sparkling with life
Seek her always, her friendship, before it is gone.

Jenny Brown
ENGLAND

Jenny was born in apartheid South Africa, where her parents were active in the ANC. Her family moved to London after her father was a political prisoner in The Old Fort, the Johannesburg prison for White men. South Africa and politics have remained important to Jenny throughout her life. She began writing poetry and songs in her twenties, was an active education campaigner for decades, and was twice interviewed on *Newsnight*. Jenny took Open University courses, while working as a teaching assistant and becoming a teacher herself aged 50. Since retirement in 2014, Jenny has contributed to local activism, dug out her shelved anthologies, and joined a local poetry writing group. Her poems are influenced by nature, relationships and injustice. Jenny enjoys writing poems that reveal, as well as those that heal.

E: jenny29brown@hotmail.co.uk

WANTING YOU TO KNOW

It's not a matter of taking the moral high-ground,
Ricocheting blades of blame around.
It's not a matter of not trying to turn things around.
Forces came along saying I cannot stay.
Into the frame came a dark dirty way.
I am letting go, eventually.

I was fated to meet that reckless lady,
I saw her heavy artillery,
Heard whispers of caution regularly.
Yet, tempted by a poisoned chalice,
I landed in her web of ego status.
Your friendship was my life raft.

Your texts, your voice, your patience, your laugh,
Kept on saying it will be alright,
Shifted my gloom, gave light.
Your friendship keeps me upright.
Letting go was the best way to be.
Wanting you to know how precious your friendship is to me.

WHY?

You said grey was best.
I said, green at least.
Irritation set like concrete
Disdain felt like lies,
With no clue from your eyes,
I realised our breakup was being finalised.
Christmas saw upsets lingering,
Whispers sparked flickering,
Outpourings of reverberating ripples became ferocious waves.
This is not how we used to behave.
Confused anger expressed in final statements,
Clogged channels, sprinkling sadness.

Seeing bluebells beneath blossom, beneath blue sky,
My mind returns to "why"?
Crisps lost their crunch,
Calendars missed months,
Autumn colours withheld their glow,
Waiting for me to know.
Hearing reassurances that time will heal,
Brought all the hurt to subtly reveal,
A slow, steady shredding of pieces of pain,
Away from logic, towards my self to reclaim.
Bit by bit, reaching beyond and above
Waiting to make up, wanting to be brave enough.

Masudul Hoq
BANGLADESH

Masudul has a PhD in Aesthetics under Professor Hayat Mamud at Jahangirnagar University, Dhaka. He is a contemporary Bengali poet, short story writer, translator and researcher. His previous published work includes short stories; *Tamakbari* (1999), *The poems Dhonimoy Palok* (2000), *Dhadhashil Chaya,* of which the translated version is *Shadow of Illusion* (2005), and *Jonmandher Swapna*, of which the translated version is *Blind Man's Dream* (2010, translated by Kelly J. Copeland). Masudul has also translated from English to Bengali T.S. Eliot's poem *Four Quartets* (2012), and Allen Ginsburg's poem *Howl* (2018). In the late 1990s, Masudul worked for three years under a research fellowship at The Bangla Academy, which has published his two research books. His poems have been published in the Chinese, Romanian, Mandarin, Azarbaijanese, Turkish, Nepali and Spanish languages. At present he is a Professor of Philosophy at a government college.
E: masudul.hoq@gmail.com

NARCISSUS COMPLEX

I have a mirror
I hid it in the blue trunk of my childhood

When I feel bad, I go to the mirror
I can see you when I look in the mirror
This is how you and I became friends

Your face is impossibly beautiful
Your eyes are wise
I became your fan

One day I went to touch you
The mirror gets broken.

Out of that
My real face has come in front.

Prafull Shiledar
INDIA

Prafull is an eminent Marathi language poet-translator from Central India, and Chief Editor of a well known Marathi literary journal *Yugvani*. He has three poetry collections in Marathi, and one in Hindi. Translations of his poems are published in many languages including Malayalam, Gujarati, Telugu, Manipuri, English, German, Slovak and Czech. He has read poetry in many national and international poetry festivals and literary events in India, Europe, USA and Dubai, and in 2013 he was invited for poetry reading in 11th Ars Poetica International Poetry Festival, Bratislava, Slovakia. Prafull has written short stories, book reviews, film appreciations, interviews, travelogue and criticism, and is the recipient of a number of awards for his poetry, as well as for his translations including Sahitya Akademi Award by National Academy of Letters, New Delhi.
E: shiledarprafull@gmail.com
FB:@prafull.shiledar

MEETING

A poem for last meeting with poet-friend Bhujang Mehsram.
Translation by Dilip Chavan

On my return
after dropping the poet in a train
Whistling harshly
the train tries to bring me back to the senses

Suddenly its wheels begin to move
The poets pale eyes
shine at the time of farewell
a slight glitter of being lost shivers in the eyes

He looks for the support of words
while drowning and shaking about
in the water of his body

The train departs
Even before I stop thinking about
that how would he reach up to the last station
We do not even realize
that the journey of the train is so long

He came fully prepared
Heartily he embraced me
at the time of departure
He met me
compensating all those long lost days
He met me
compensating the time forever

He met me like a drop of water
in the beak of a thirsty bird
landing at the spring of water

Igor Pop Trajkov
REPUBLIC OF NORTH MACEDONIA

Igor is renowned international writer, film director and multi-disciplinary artist from North Macedonia. He has participated in many literary contests including 'Viaggi di versi' and 'Il mio libro,' and, as a film director, has made a number of short films, documentaries, music videos, commercials as well as one feature film. His theoretical works about visual arts and cinema have been published in universities including the Catholic University of Leuven and Harvard. Igor speaks eight languages, and his writings have been extensively translated internationally and he is currently working on his second PhD at the Institute of Macedonian Literature.
E: igorpoptrajkov@yahoo.com
W: www.pyramidusd.wordpress.com
FB: @Igor-Pop-Trajkov
Instagram: @trajkovpop

PRESENCE

Translated and versified from Macedonian into English by the author
Igor Pop Trajkov.

I didn't know about you my friend,
I don't know who or from where you are
(And the people in this area thought and
They will think - who knows what you are?).
I don't even know who or where you are
Now too, but I miss you a lot.

I saw you at those so-called seminars
with stinking students dragged from provinces.
And from all those in rags, when I saw you
in the overcrowded hall, my eye was caught by you.
That was in the early 1990s,
and you had worn-out jeans too
with cleft knee. And you were with plenty of zeal
as all others you imitated G. Michael.
But when I saw you, this one seemed stupid to me
since I don't know why this seemed to me
more than life. Someone must have given those
jeans for you to wear them in front of others. Whereas
I actually didn't look at you much, I thought you were
behind me and waiting for everything to pass firstly,
but then I felt that you had in everything
your share; you are not without a goal. Thinking
just then we were in our best years,
but how unfortunate, only wars
were happening around us. We wanted
to travel, but we weren't allowed, and
we couldn't, we were too poor. And
you, kind of, with all this even than
were reconciled. Always in your own
film entered.

Life is shaken
and then continues. Every young adult
the comrade sought in himself unique.
I felt like you were lonely too, whereas
not like me, left to the nightmares.
I didn't know who was frightening you, who was comforting.
But you never complained; with this you were never mistaking.
He was wisely silent with his contemptuous identity

ascended in his duration, not expectation
of the better which never arrives.
Eh, I thought, I wish could do it like you
cold-bloodedly keep myself silenced about the hypocritical
gatherings, of the corrupt students.
Your beginning was the end of the purchased
revolution; bought with scholarships
p. party booklets, love of the racketeers
G. Michael's jeans, love for the racketeers.
That's how we ended up with criminalities.
Where are you now? did you succeed? and now
I don't know anything about you. As I know
not from what I lost all somehow.
And maybe it wasn't easy for you either?
I remember how much coffee you drank in American style
although you smelled on cheap pindjur, all in gypsy style.
Cup handed in your sausage fingers,
and then - sip! and only you are different, and all others
are same. I miss your Englishness
in having a point, and your hand over my shoulder while
joint tripping. When you disappeared all disappeared.
Only the cheap smell of the canteen
stayed ...
Presence, that's something spiritual.
Call me, please, just do it. You have me.
It's like that all the time, it's all alone for me.

First published in *Songs from Death and Love*, Scribd. 2016.

CHILD FOREVER (REMEMBER)

Translated and versified from Macedonian into English by the author
Igor Pop Trajkov.

Although he wasn't very
old he didn't feel like living.
All time he was just silent and
when someone asking
he would say: "All night headache
I was having, I couldn't be speaking."
And less and less human word he heard,
for always he gave the same answer;
the one said above and people thought
that he wants to hide as through
his secret he was tormented. But none
knew that this exactly was the one
why he was good, as he spoke to nobody
nor anyone spoke to him. He knew
he also has no friends
nor for everyone worthy advice,
but he missed the child
in him. Now already the doorstep
of the old age is reaching so mild,
thinking not of youth, but childhood.
So that when dead, before
to say to himself to remember:
"I am a child forever".

First published in *Songs from Death and Love*, Scribd. 2016.

Rosy Gallace
ITALY

Since her youth, Rosy cultivated a passion for writing poetry and stories. In 2011, she participated in national and international literary contests and won numerous prestigious awards, including the Culture Award in 2014. In the same year, she was evaluated by Professor Michele Cattaneo - the Mayor of the city of Rescaldina - for her commitment to culture. Rosy is the creator, organizer, and president of several literary contests and poetry reading sessions, along with book presentations, and juries various literary competitions. Her works have been included in several anthologies of contemporary poetry, and has published four books of poetry: *Small fragments, Remaining days, Unspoken words*, and T*races of memory*. Moreover, she is a singer in Rescaldina's Santa Cecilia Choir, has acted in the presentation of the theatre opera: *Shadows of tormented memory*, written and directed by the poet, writer, and producer Fabiano Braccini in memory of the victims in the Nazi concentration camps, and voluntarily teaches the Italian language to foreigners.
E: rosygallace@gmail.com

PETALS OF LIGHT
Translated from Italian into English by Irma Kurti.

I stole from the wind
the sighs of blossoming
flowers for you.

I caught an eagle's flight
that smelled of rock
in the clear source of a limpid
and windy April morning.

I'll be a grain of wheat for you
that on the clods of my silence
will be reborn to be an ear.

I'll steal dust from the moon,
fragments from the stars
to illuminate your way.

With patience, I will weave
in your heart diadems of light
that you'll admire lightly,
like petals of roses
in the garden of your days.

I'll walk in the footsteps of your journey,
I will face your gaze,
proud and sincere, I will wait for you,
where the sun never sets,
and I will offer you a dawn
dressed only in hope.

IN A TIME TO COME
Translated from Italian into English by Irma Kurti.

On winter evenings
when you'll sing the lullaby,
you will recite the nursery rhymes,
you'll tuck a baby's blankets.
In that instant, I will be.

When you will accompany him
in his first uncertain steps,
and you'll read his first notes in the diary.

When you will seat around a large table
for the Christmas holidays
and you will taste kneaded sweets
with dried figs, walnuts, and chopped almonds.
That's when you'll remember me.

When in the evenings you'll wait behind a window
the late coming home of a boy.
In the bright red of the embers
of a lit fireplace,
in the toasted slices of bread
seasoned with good oil and the scent of oregano.
That's where you will find me.

I call to my mind your revisiting
the places of my childhood.
Between the lines of this yellowed sheet
that you just found behind that wardrobe
… and then …
In every beat of your heart,
as often as you'll want,
in that time, I'll be.

THE EXPIRED TIME
Translated from Italian into English by Irma Kurti.

It wasn't the highway kilometres
that made us feel distant.
It wasn't the labour
or the cost of the tolls.

It wasn't even
a round trip on an *easyJet*.
It was our thoughts
so distant ... and ... different.

Our time has travelled
between parallel lives
chasing each other, never meeting.

Our thoughts intertwined
with the days filled with loneliness;
now, they're here in their nakedness.

Our time has expired.

For once, without finding any holds,
let's look at each other through sincere
eyes and beyond words, let us listen
to the rhythms of heart, let's shake
hands, be real, let's just be ourselves.

Suchismita Ghoshal

INDIA

Suchismita hails from West Bengal. With an academic career in science, she is currently pursuing her masters in business administration (MBA) from GD Goenka University in Gurgaon, Haryana. At just 23 years-old, Suchismita is also a professional multi-award winning writer, published author, internationally acclaimed poet, literary critic, literary influencer, content writing member for the West Bengal United Nations Youth Association, the International Organisation Of United Nations Volunteers, and the Helping Hand International Organisation. With more than 520 coveted co-authorship in various renowned national and international anthologies, prestigious literary magazines, websites, webzines and eminent literary journals and have been translated into Arabic and Italian. She has also authored three poetry books by the name of *Fields of Sonnet*, *Poetries in Quarantine* and *Emotions & Tantrums*.
E: ghoshalsuchismita019@gmail.com
W: www.suchismitaghoshal.com
FB: @suchismita.ghoshal.96,
Instagram: @storytellersuchismita
Wordpress: www.creativesuchi.wordpress.com

TALES OF OUR FRIENDSHIP

When the nights engross me,
with love, laughter & lullabies.
I only recall the solace,
only can come if we had met with each other.
Crossing my legs with an empty heart & null soul,
I see the glittering stars of winter sky,
I witness the rain draining the sky in monsoon,
I observe the silent sobs of summer sky,
I miss us, I miss our togetherness with all my heart.
Though the mild breeze flows touching my skin,
I feel the miracle, miracle of your presence;
as it mesmerises & soothes my thoughts.
I walk by a riverside while watching the ripples of it,
noticing the reflection it draws & they recall you two.
Even the chirping birds & the beautiful meadows,
wrench my heart touching the deepest corner of it
where we three are residing only, with all the joys & glees.
I see the air bubbles floating in the air,
they blabber your names & set my desire on fire.
I want to face your mischievous talks & soulful laughs,
while i have to remain with the photos & heartfelt glooms.
People say I have a better flair in poetry,
& I think the reason lies in you two.
The way you guys make me laugh & lighten my mood up,
the way you guys uplift in my down periods,
& the way you leave your footprints imprinted in my soul
tells the 'tales of our friendship', irreplaceable.
I still wait for the day we will meet,
& flush out our emotions while bursting out into cries,
embracing each other like a thread, unsplittable;
& will shout out about the 'tales of our friendship' to my world of
scribbles.

FRIENDSHIP

Years passed away,
School days faded away,
College days stumbled upon on the finishing line,
Days waved 'goodbye',
& golden moments turned into mere memories.
But the friends we left behind
Still beckon us for a gossip over a cup of chai,
For a sudden trip on the hills of joy,
For an instant mood swing in a lonesome evening,
Or for a break in our monotonous life.
Friends feel like the season of spring,
As they reverberates the tunes of a guitar string,
Our shenanigans chant the new mantras of living,
Songs are the friends whereas lyrics are the tales of our togetherness
On a mysterious journey called 'life',
We need our friends to be as nomad as us to
strengthen our basics.
Some stories, too confidential to be shared,
Are only enjoyed by the friends for a strange trust.
Some stories, too unique to be shared with any random,
Are relished by the friends for a recreation of memories.
Friendship means loyalty when you cherish it,
Friendship feels honest when you give all of it,
Friendship brings care when you know how to care
& friendship recalls love when you fly in the air.
Obstructions come & pushed back to return
Only when your friend fight for you ;
Vivacious, compassionate, mesmerising & strong,
Friendship is a compact package for lifelong.
We are so blind without our mates
as our friendship are one of their own kind,
Every single day & every single night,
When the stars shimmer so bright,
We search for our lost companions over the sky.
God knows if they still miss our vines,
When we gladly used to spend our time,
Hours & minutes count our age,
Rapidly increasing like a ladder
& growing old in our own life-stage.
As long as we breath for the last time,
There'll be wishes to meet our old love;
The love of school friends & their stories

When we cried & laughed at the same time
in our friendship's glory.

Shaswata Gangopadhyay
INDIA

Born and bought up in Kolkata, and graduating in Science and Corporate Management, Shaswata started writing poetry in the mid-'90s, and is now one of the prominent faces of contemporary Bengali poetry. Shaswata has exhibited at the Poetry Festival in Picollo Museum, Italy, and has participated in a large number of poetry festivals across Europe and the USA. His poetry has been published in all the major journals of Bengali literature, and has been translated into English and published in journals and anthologies in Europe, America, Asia, Africa and Latin America. His book of poems are: *Inhabitant of Pluto Planet* (2001), *Offspring of Monster* (2009) and *Holes of Red Crabs* (2015).
E: shaswatagangopadhyay@gmail.com
FB: @shaswata.gangopadhyay.7

THE FRIEND
Translated by Rajdeep Mukherjee

'A man is all alone when, instead of a bridge,
He constructs a hard wall around both of his sides.'

Wrote a Greek philosopher in his diary.
Myself also etched a long tattoo on the palms of my hands,
The name of my dear friend,his latest phone number.
In the scorching heat of noon,when my tongue gets dry,
After walking a long way on the pitched road,
With my slipper-straps torn,
I enter a booth and pick up the receiver to make him a call.

Oh,if I could slake my thirst with a green coconut,
In one sip on my straw-lips.

Arpita Sam
BAHRAIN / INDIA

Arpita is a writer/poet/artist and an aspiring high-school student whose passion is spending her time writing poetry and reading. Her achievements include winning numerous international poetry and astronomy Olympiad accolades. Apart from physics and poetry, she also loves math, reading, Carl Sagan, and Cosmos - her adopted cat.

AFFINITY ANCHORS

I was 11 when she said I looked feeble,
And seized her book away
You filched it from my dresser
She evermore used to say

She never really bothered about me
She was an A-star model kid, ms. perfect.
Her stance was quite vaguely brackish
Sitting beside her gave me the quakes.

I couldn't help steal that novel yet again,
It was sitting, solemn on her desk
Never touched, never tussled, never folded,
Simply in want, come on, I was delirious.

She stood aghast, that word rhymes her surname
As I completed half of the book in a succinct time
Who knew that was my ultimatum
That thirst for utter knowledge was my affinity anchor.

She glorified my nimble brain
My fleet sinewy fingers
My indeed swifter pupils, that dilated information
I cowered in constrained pride.

Oh captain, my captain,
Those days we crooned and masqueraded.
We consigned and snickered,
And shared exam profit intrigues

We were soon best friends,
Clinging together, and refusing to part
Would I never have such a companion,
If I didn't read that book, that was on the dresser, like a hawk?

Chrys Salt MBE
ENGLAND / SCOTLAND

Based between London and Edinburgh, Chrys is a seasoned performer and a widely published and anthologized poet. She has performed in festivals across the UK, in Europe, America, Canada, Finland and India, and written in almost every genre except the novel. Numerous awards include a National Media Award, an Arts and Business Award, Several Writing Bursaries and a Fringe First from The Edinburgh Festival. She has published seven books for actors, and nine poetry collections. She is Artistic Director of BIG LIT: The Stewartry Book Festival, a five day literary festival in SW Scotland now in its ninth year. Chrys was awarded an MBE in the Queen's Birthday Honours List for Services to The Arts.
E: chrys@chryssalt.com
W: www.chryssalt.com
W: www.biglit.org

CAROL IN JUNIORS

Tasselled with ringlets
was Carol in Juniors.
Bum big as Birmingham.
Face like a gibbon.
Carol in Juniors
pinned up and parcelled
with butterfly hair slides
and satiny ribbon.
Puckered and dimpled
all over with smocking.
socks that were star-bright.
Socks never dropping.
Me, in my hand-me-down
Liberty bodice
jumpers re-knitted
from several-hand wool.
God, how I hated her,
Carol in Juniors!
Carol whose mum
always came up to school.

Eduard Schmidt-Zorner
REPUBLIC OF IRELAND / GERMANY

Eduard is a translator and writer of poetry, haibun, haiku and short stories, also under his pen-name Eadbhard McGowan. He writes in four languages: English, French, Spanish and German, and is published in over 140 anthologies, literary journals and broadsheets in the USA, the UK, Ireland, Japan, Sweden, Spain, Italy, Bangladesh, India, France, Mauritius, Nepal, Pakistan, Nigeria and Canada. Eduard holds workshops on Japanese and Chinese style poetry and prose, and experimental poetry, and some of his poems and haibun have been published in French (own translation), Romanian and Russian. Member of four writer groups in Ireland, and lives in County Kerry for more than 25 years, Eduard is a proud Irish citizen, born in Germany.
E: EadbhardMcGowan@gmx.com

DISTANT FRIENDSHIP

She met *Vladimir* once in *East-Berlin*,
fell in love, spent time with him.
He was a handsome junior lieutenant,
but this German-Russian friendship,
though a communist dream,
was not well accepted.

He was, for disciplinary reasons,
transferred to near the river *Lena*,
9000 km from Moscow, far Siberia,
to quench this flame of friendship,
kill this young luck,
prevent fraternization.

No sign of life from him, no letter,
not a word, decades passed.
As soon as communism fell,
she made a journey along the *Lena*
to see to where he was exiled,
his place of banishment.

To share with him, invisibly,
his country's glowing atmosphere,
the vast expanse, endless horizon,
with him to be united
in the divine depth of his land.

Is it him, there on the bench,
in front of a wooden house?
White-haired, with broken empty heart?
She waves at him, just in case.
The ship's orchestra plays
the song of the *'Sacred War'*.

Dreamy, seeing the banks pass by,
dark green, emerald, bright green,
the red gold yellow sunset.
Still him in mind,
so near, but still so far away.

Rodavgi Gkogkoni
GREECE

Rodavgi is a graduate of Pedagogy Studies in Primary Education, as well as a graduate of Computer Science. Poetry is, and has always been, an important aspect of her life. She is a member of the International Union of Greek Literary Writers and Artists, and participated in the Worldwide Forum of Virtual Poetry in Tunisia, alongside 173 other poets from all over the world. In 2019 she published her first poetry collection *Loving Moonlight*.
E: rgkogkoni@gmail.com
FB: @gkogkoni

HATE KILLS US

Translated into English by Vasiliki Kalahani Korinthia.

If I knew this world better
What they seek and
What they ask
Without using their mind
Oh ... how much
do they want to estimate
everything here?

I wanted a heart from a relative
And a heart from a friend too
Souls to photograph
Which one would look
Like honey from a bee?
And which one would look
Like teeth from a dog?

The friend feels pain
The relative buries you
With jealousy and lies
The bad one takes you
To Hade's dark night

They don't know
They don't realize
That our time is ending
That everything here
Will be left
Oh ... this awful hate
How terribly it is killing us!

Maid Čorbić
BOSNIA AND HERZEGOVINA

Maid is 21 years-old and from Tuzla. In his spare time he writes poetry. He is a member of the WLFPH (World Literature Forum Peace and Humanity), and the editor of the portal *First Virtual Space Olympic*, led by Dijana Uherek Stevanović, which aims to connect poets around the world. Maid's poetry has also been published in anthologies and magazines worldwide including in: Chile, Spain, Ecuador, San Salvador, United Kingdom, Indonesia, India, Croatia and Serbia, as well as in printed anthologies including *Sea in the palm of your hand*, *Stories from Isolation*, *Kosovo Peony* and others. In 2020, he was named the poet of the year by the Indo-Universe group, which is also engaged in charity work around the world.
E: detrix233@gmail.com
FB: @xcelendge
Instagram: @zaglavlje

FRIENDS ARE ALWAYS HERE

You should never turn away from your friends
Who are always there with you always
Because happiness is greater when we have those people
Which we know all my life

Everything can be changed easily
And that people fade with age
But certainly the importance of life is to have people
Stick to and stay away from the Internet

We do not need to be stiff and dependent
Because it creates the intoxicating thread and core of life
Which doesn't really have a beginning
But not even their end, friends are always there

Don't underestimate anyone, because they are human after all
They really like to be happy
And nothing else is left to do again
Let's support everyone around us, those wonderful friends

They protect us from all evil
They believe that everything will be fine
And that there is a reason for another celebration
Valuable for life, and irreplaceable

Daniela Andonovska-Trajkovska
REPUBLIC OF NORTH MACEDONIA

Daniela is a poet, scientist, editor, literary critic, doctor of pedagogy, and university professor. She is co-founder of the University Literary Club Denicija PFBT UKLO, and also of the Center for Literature, Art, Culture, Rhetoric and Language at the Faculty of Education - Bitola. She is a member of the Macedonian Writers' Association, and The Bitola Literary Circle, and was president of the Macedonian Science Society Editorial Council (for two mandates). She is editor-in-chief of the literary journal *Rast/Growth* (Bitola Literary Circle), editor-in-chief of the International Journal *Contemporary Dialogues* (Macedonian Science Society), and editor of *Literary Elements Journal* (Perun Artis), as well as several poetry and prose books. Besides her scientific work (over 100 published scientific articles) and a university book titled *Critical Literacy*, she writes poetry, prose and literary critics. She has published one prose book *Coffee, Tea and the Red Sky* (2019), co-authored one poetry book for children, and eight poetry books: *Word about the Word* (2014), *Poems for the Margins* (2015), *Black Dot* (2017), *Footprints* (2017), *Three* (2019), *House of Contrasts* (2019), *Electronic Blood* (2019), and *Math Poetry* (2020). She has won special mention at the Nosside World Poetry Prize (UNESCO, 2011), and a number of other prestigious awards including the national award for poetry Aco Shopov (by Macedonian Writers' Association in 2021 for the book *Math Poetry*). Her poetry has been published in a large number of anthologies, literary magazines and journals both at home and abroad, and translated into almost 20 languages.
E: daniela.andonovska@uklo.edu.mk

PERPENDICULAR LINES

the crystal cells are moving unnoticeably
on the life line
the planes perpendicularly cut my body
in infinite number of points
and I got stomach pain

I have friends that lurk in the shadows
and crucify me on two perpendicular lines
to be what I should become
- the best version of myself

Borche Panov
REPUBLIC OF NORTH MACEDONIA

Borche graduated in Macedonian and South Slavic Languages from the Sts. Cyril and Methodius University of Skopje, and has been a member of the Macedonian Writers' Association since 1998. His published poetry includes *What did Charlie Ch. See from the Back Side of the Screen* (1991), *Cyclone Eye* (1995), *Stop, Charlie* (2002), *Tact* (2006), *The Riddle of Glass* (2008), *Basilica of Writing* (2010), *Mystical Supper* (2012), *Vdah* (*The Breathe of Life*) (2014), *Human Silences* (2016), *Uhania* (2017), *Shell* (2018); and several essays and plays: *The Fifth Season of the Year* (2000), *The Doppelgänger Town* (2011), *A Dead-end in the Middle of an Alley* (2002), *Homo Soapiens* (2004), *Catch the Sleep-walker* (2005), *Split by its own Nose* (2006), and *Summertime Cinema* (2007). He has also poetry books published in other languages including *Particles of Hematite* (2016-in Macedonian and Bulgarian, published in Bulgaria), *Vdah* (2017 – in Slovenian, published in Slovenia), *Balloon Shaving* (2018 – Serbian, published in Serbia), *Fotostiheza* (*Photopoesis*, 2019 – Bulgarian, published in Bulgaria), *Blood that Juggles with 80000 Thoughts* (2021 - in Croatian, published in Croatia). His poetry was published in a number of anthologies, literary magazines and journals, both at home and abroad, and his works are translated into English, Ukrainian, Slovenian, Bosnian, Serbian, Croatian, Bulgarian, French, Catalonian, Mongolian, Uzbek, Albanian, Romanian, Polish, Italian, Arabic, Vietnamese, Chinese, and Danish language. Panov works as a Counsellor for Culture and Education at the municipality of Radovish, and Arts Coordinator for the International Karamanov's Poetry Festival, held in Radovish annually.
E: borcepanov@yahoo.com
FB: @borce.panov

THE NIGHT FACE OF THE SUN
Translated from Macedonian into English by Prof. Dr. Daniela
Andonovska-Trajkovska.

When the apples were ripening with the morning light,
and when the palm was ripening around the apple as well,
the apples were also ripening quietly with the full moon
that was showing to us the face of the Sun in the gloom

When a lightening broke into the old house
like a heated apple, and grandpa opened the windows
to prevent it to hit the walls of the poor little rooms and said
that a free soul shouldn't be stopped

When the carps were jumping out of the calm water
splashing the moon in circles of vocals
when a human landed on the Moon for the first time
and bounced free from the gravity and the weight of the mind

When I and my friend from my childhood, Elijah
were laying down on the back and we were thinking loudly with the
stars bright
and we were looking at the infinite diamond of the cosmos
grinded in innumerable angles that flash with the whole time

When we started to crave to keep our time safe
in one flight even before we spread our wings,
and we didn't know that we were threat to ourselves
and the life and the death were not enough to each other

When our palms finished ripening around the apple
and the apples were ripening quietly with the full moon,
you showed us peacefully, dear God, the night face of the Sun
as a fruit that does not get picked by the unspoken perfection

Anna Banasiak
POLAND

Anna is an award winning poet, literary critic and occupational therapist. Her poems have been published in New York, London, Australia, Canada, India, Africa, Japan, China and Israel. She has had many books published including *Duet of Tears* - English-Japanese poetry book co-authored with Noriko Nagaoka, *Duet of Waves* - an English-Japanese poetry book co-authored with Yoshimasa Kanou, and *Duet of Masks – an* English-Persian poetry book co-authored with Afrooz Yafarinoor.
E: banama7@wp.pl

INSOMNIA

quiet rhythms of jazz
flow in the pouring rain
we cuddle the pillow
my dog and I
lonely jazzmen
we fall
in the bliss
of freedom

Ewith Bahar
INDONESIA

Ewith is a poet, novelist, translator and essayist, and lives in Jakarta. She had a long time career in the mass-communication, radio and television industry as a TV host at *Television of Republic of Indonesia* for several cultural and musical programs. One of her poetry books, *Sonata Borobudur*, got a prestigious prize from Indonesian National Library as The Best Five Indonesian Poetry Books 2019. She has published nine books, in all genres; poetry, short stories, novel and essay. Ewith also loves teaching, and taught at the Communication Institution, Interstudi and LEPPKINDO, and a public speaker for communications matters, creative writing and bibliotherapy.
E: ewith2408@yahoo.com
E: edbawythona04@gmail.com
FB: @Ewith.Bahar

THE DAY YOU'RE GONE

From a half-opened window
My eyes touched the wide horizon
Pondering the flying days, missing moments, and all memories about
you,
which stretches out
A treasure that will live forever

On the epitaph, elegy I wrote
will never decay
But the bitterness and pain of losing you
will always stay

The day I left the pale you
and the pale hospital room
Your eyes followed
as I went out and waved
And two hours later, my phone rang
from the hospital ...
My tears wetting the receiver.

Jean E. Ragual
SINGAPORE / PHILIPPINES

Jean's work has been featured in the Migrant Workers Photography Festival 2019, won the 'Places and Architecture' category. Jean was also finalist of Migrant Worker Poetry Competition, Singapore, 2017 and overall winner Unspoken Life Photography Competition, 2020.
E: jeanragual@gmail.com
FB: @100015462605963

TRUE FRIEND

Take the flow of life
whether one hand hang,
hauling a depressed friend,
stop and go with them.

Don't know what to expect,
but knowing that everything is finite,
at least it looks good
little by little the fulfilment of the prospect.

Even the stones in the path of the stream
Can turn the river's flow aside.
And obstacles in your way
May make you lose heart.

Just keep flowing,
even though many are criticizing
obstruct a specific command,
make sure always faithful to God.

Part of human life;
choose your own preferences,
be content,
because the one you love is good enough.

Jelena Zagorac
SERBIA

Jelena graduated in Comparative Literature and writes poems and short stories. She is represented in different magazines and collections including *Poezija zlatnih stihova 2* (*Poetry of Golden Verse 2*) published by *Pici i književnost - Writers and Literature, Litterateur: Redefining world,* and online literary magazine *Enheduana*, published by The Association for Promotion of Cultural Diversity Alia Mundi. As the contributor of the Association, in 2020 she took part in Festival of Hope organized by Versopolis, and supported by Creative Europe Programme of the European Union. Since 2018, she writes and edits her personal blog.

E: jecazagorac@gmail.com
W: www.jelenazagorac.wordpress.com
FB: @jelena.zagorac.10
Instagram: @jecazagorac
Linkedin: @jelena-zagorac-b47778a0

A WISH
To my best friend.

At the time I really used to hate my body.
And it seems I really wished for something bad to happen to my friends, too.
And then ...
The summer was hot – the Danube was cold. The dawn was breaking – one young life decided to end itself.
Eight months later I saw her crying. And how she kept apologizing.
As if she was committing a sin. She remained silent in her pain. As if she was committing a sin.
Only later have I have realized that it was the first time I have seen my best friend crying.
I have wished for – and it was fulfilled.
Now I only wish to hug her and that everything becomes all right again.
I have wished for – and it was fulfilled.
I will wish for one more time. It might be fulfilled.

Meenakshi Palaniappan
SINGAPORE

Meenakshi is a Literature educator by profession, and a quiet observer of the world around her. She writes to think, and enjoys playing with words to paint pictures of life as she sees it. Initially she took to writing partly to cope with this pain of separation, but now she mainly writes about her children and family, as well as nature. Her poems have been published online in *The Tiger Moth Review, Shot Glass Journal* and *Mothers Always Write*.
E: meena3.saro@gmail.com
FB: @MeenakshiPalaniappan

WHAT IS FRIENDSHIP BUT...
For Malar, my best friend of 30 years.

... us giggling under an umbrella
on the way to the bus stop
the rain drenching us anyway;

us whispering to each other
in the school hall at assembly
till we are sent out to stand at the back;

us chatting non-stop
as we run around the field
at hockey practice;

us analysing song lyrics
for innuendos, making them up
when there were none;

us calling the other without fail
on the stroke of midnight
on our birthdays;

us waiting for the other,
hours on end if need be,
for there must be a good reason;

us forgiving each other
the hurt we caused,
the words spoken out of turn;

us wiping the other's tears
after each heartbreak,
never forgiving the guy;

us hearing that song on the radio
and bobbing in tune, recalling
our dancing days at *Kilimanjaro**;

us saying the things
the other needs to hear
even if we would rather not listen;

us picking up from a conversation

just like yesterday,
even if months have rolled by;

us holding fast to the other,
even if oceans swell between us
today.

*A dancing club that was popular in the late '90s in Singapore.

FRIENDS LIKE PEARLS

I collect my friends
like freshwater pearls over time -
an amulet.
Now they scatter across the table.
I wait to thread us together again.

Gabriella Garofalo
ITALY

Born in Italy some decades ago, at age just six, Gabriella both fell in love with the English language and started writing poems in Italian She has contributed to a number of national and international magazines and anthologies, and is the author of *Lo sguardo di Orfeo, L'inverno di vetro, Di altre stelle polari, Casa di erba, Blue branches* and *A Blue Soul*.
E: grrz2001@yahoo.it

FRIENDSHIP?

No way, was it the moon who used to be her friend,
To strike her with light,
Just to ice those fingers starving for heat -
Do they trust your hands, by the by?
Two strings in tune swing together, or so they say,
But when one gets hurt,
Her sister can't play the same song, right?
C'mon, drop it now, dear moon, your friend
Slashes the names women threw up,
The dark sound of a womb -
Meanwhile, she hips you to life,
To dazzle her friends, shadows, waves,
The whole shebang -
Bit funny, I mean, innit?
Meanwhile, lost among blasting comets, aisles, swindles, You hear
'em hissing 'round
"Wow, what a swanky resort for loss 'n' desire" -
So, stop it now, as she isn't up to soothing you -
Your darling dearest friend, naked and blue,
Slinks up on you, just like your soul -
No use, of course, hidden somewhere in the attic,
Children, teens, grass, trees,
All missing, all gone, and you listen now,
Only walls, words, and books befriend my light,
So, get some, my soul,
Scrape by, c'mon, weave among
Those shattered cars hailing from the jaws of Cerberus -
What else, her third friend, a bastard town
Hotbed of desire, will get by just about,
If the scribe twists papers, smiles at blue lights,
Stumps all the songs dreaming of slaking
Thirst in deepest friendship, of course -
Hold on, and beware of those friends,
Steer clear of dark alleys and lousy stars.
See? Lovers too smile dark and grim
When deadbolts jilt the keys,
They can't be swayed, simple as that,
While withering limbs and rakes
get busy stalking prey.
Oh, lest I forget, something for all tastes,
A thingy for all and sundry, you know?
The blue fire no love no word can silence,

Maybe silent lovers, or, who knows,
Red-hot old growlers thriving on
Drugs, surgery, treatments, and bigwigs.
But look at how vulnerable the sky is:
An infinite frailty of stars, maybe comets.

Lindsay Walter
ENGLAND

Lindsay lives in York. She likes small round white crystal stones.
Empty spaces, even underground, damp and chilly. Time to herself.
Quiet. Quantum. Jung. And listening to intuition.
E: lindsay.walter@gmail.com

WHERE YOU WERE

i don't know where you were
when you died
'suicide' someone said
i wrote to your mother

for a while at school
in Malton
we were friends
i remember you in uniform
sky blue and navy
head down shoulders squared
in a hurry
i did like you

we squabbled in Art
squashed each other's
clay pigs
agreed where babies came from
disagreed
on where they came out
liked each other
then grew apart

you spent weekends
in Newcastle
never said
what you did what you'd done

at college
in Totley
you broke down
lost your place

i glimpsed you sedated
on a ward
in York
you weren't really there
you turned up
in Cherry Hinton
on a motorbike in leathers
someone called the police

in London
you had an abortion
your mother came
to care

you got married lived
in Slough
three tiny children
i saw them sleeping once

i heard you gave away
one of your twins 'you
can't hold hands
with three' you'd said

i don't know
where you were
when you killed yourself

Newcastle perhaps

Keith Jepson
ENGLAND

Keith is a Fine Art, History of Art and Philosophy graduate, and has been running his own Sports Marketing and PR consultancy for 13 years. He writes for the press in the cycling industry, and has had his poems and columns published in local and regional magazines. His work covers varied subjects from landscapes, places he has visited, the loss of sight in my left eye, Salopian landscapes and the death of his Father.
E: team@maxbikespr.co.uk

FRIENDSHIP

Friends are like the tides or seasons.

Changing but constant. Always there, like a warm shadow.

Clothed in a blanket, lofty love leaves, friends are the shelter of trees.

A domain of truth. True friends are never distant, but can be far away and away for a long time,

like an ancient Albatross. Not like a weighty Coleridge bird, but a faithful lookout, watchful of our tides.

Friends are the colourful fresco's that surround us.

They are the flying buttresses that support our fragile walls.

They have a seat in our head, at our star chamber. They are our cornerstone of

checks and balances, our moral media.

With a light hand on our shoulder, pushing down or propping up.

Like slow moving clouds, ever present, somewhere.

Friends are the wind of memory, your own zephyr pushing warmth westward.

Like riding a full stop Tandem. Stoker or pilot, lead or be led they ride the same

journey.

The ships on the horizon are captained by them. They are Pans shadow, they lead us to and welcome us at

Peter's Gate.

They are the pale moon rising and the golden sun setting.

They are in the hour of light and Goya's darkness.

Friends are the piano at dawn and the strings of evening. Words are not needed.

They are in the corner of short smiles, at the edge of small glances and in the tiniest of touches.

Life's quest ... ought to be ... find as many as you can and be as many as you can!

They are Nimrod, the Lark ascending, bike rides, camp fires, cut grass, climbing flowers and fresh rain.

Folded into life's layers, woven into our tapestry and seeded in all our new growth.

At our altars, in the stained glass of our eyes. The currency of an ancient language, friends are the prize.

Seek them out.

They are our mortar.

Friendship.

Glória Sofia
CAPE VERDE

Glória has had her work published in a number of magazines and websites including *youngpoets.eu, Azahar, Miombo Publishing Lepan Africa, Edebİyat Nöbetİ, Armağan magazine, betterthanstarbucks* and *scurfpeapublishing.* She has participated in International Poetry Festivals in Romania (2016), Turkey (2017), Macedonia/Albania (2018), and has also been invited by the universities of Boston, Harvard and Tufts to read and discuss her work. Glória has also represented her country in the VIII Conference of Portuguese Language and Literature.
E: gloriasvmonteiro@gmail.com
W: gloriasvmonteiro.wixsite.com/gloriasofia
FB: @autoragloriasofia

IN YOU MY FRIEND

And when the time
crash the clock
In the remaining station
in the dream that lasts
screams are replaced
For the bitter and light look
Jumps are contained
by calm steps
sure and firm

fatigue leaves
the stomach
the rich laughs
forget the heart

All words
all laughs
all attempts
are lost
On thee
Only in you

I'm full of a
empty hope
in you my friend

Dr. Eftichia Kapardeli
GREECE

Eftichia has a Doctorate from Arts and Culture World Academy. Born in Athens and lives in Patras, she writes poetry, stories, short stories, xai-kou, essays and novels. She studied journalism at AKEM (Athenian Training Centre), and Greek culture at the University of Cyprus. She has contributed to a number of international poetry collections, and has won many awards in both national and international competitions. Eftichia is also a member of the IWA and The World Poets Society.
E: kapardeli@gmail.com
FB: @kapardeli.eftichia

FRIENDS

In parasol weather
and today's suffocation
life goes by, forgetful ...

But the soul is excess
power from kiss
of heart and debt gets

The eyes carve light
within the cycles of deprivation
pierced words on half open lips
And at bowels old red signs

Flowers expensive, only friends are left
That the wild winds
they still hold their warm tender hands

Monica Manolachi
ROMANIA

Monica is a lecturer of English and Spanish at the University of Bucharest. As a poet, she has published three collections, *Joining the Dots* (PIM, 2016), *Fragaria's Stories to Magus Viridis* (Brumar, 2012) *and Roses* (Lumen, 2007), and her poems have been published in *The Blue Nib, Artemis Poetry, Culture Cult, Crevice, Contemporary Literary Horizon* and others. In 2018, she co-authored the bilingual poetry collection *Brasília* (PIM, 2018) with Scottish poet Neil Leadbeater. *Performative Identities in Contemporary Caribbean British Poetry* (2017), is part of her work as a researcher and literary critic. She has published numerous academic articles on contemporary poetry and prose including *Multiethnic resonances in Derek Walcott's poetry*, in *Ethnic Resonances in Performance, Literature, and Identity* (2019), and *December 1989 and the concept of revolution in the prose of Romanian women writers*, in the *Swedish Journal of Romanian Studies* (2020). Over the past 15 years, she has translated various types of poetry, as well as several classical and contemporary novels into Romanian. In September 2016, her *Antologie de poezie din Caraibe* was awarded the 'Dumitru Crăciun' Prize for Translation at the International Festival Titel Constantinescu, Râmnicu Sărat. Her most recent translation project is the anthology *Over Land, Over Sea: Poems for Those Seeking Refuge* (Five Leaves, 2015). As a cultural journalist, she has published articles in local literary magazines, and the bilingual collection of interviews *Table Talk* (PIM, 2018).
E: monicamanolachi@yahoo.com
FB: @monica.manolachi
Twitter: @MonicaManolachi

RED SQUIRRELS

If you felt alone and cheerless
and wished somebody be with you
when you take walks in the park
among pushchairs and scooters in June,
and I were a red squirrel
on the branch of a wild cherry tree
when you raised your eyes unawares
and thought of foreign gardens,
I'd let a cherry drop on your shoulder
to help you clear your mind
and sigh and feel at ease and wish
there were some red squirrels
in the park where you live.

Amrita Valan
INDIA

Amrita is a writer from Bangalore, and the mother of two boys. She has a master's degree in English Literature, and has worked in the hospitality industry, several BPOs, and also as content creator for deductive logic and reasoning in English. She writes poems, essays and short stories, which have been published online in *Spillwords, ImpSpired, Potato Soup Journal, Portland Metrozine, Poetry and Places, Café Lit, Café Dissensus, Modern Literature* and *Indian Periodical,* as well as in several international anthologies.
E: amritavalan@gmail.com
FB: @amritavalan

MY CHILDHOOD FRIEND

My friend she loved me
Spoilt me to death
On the school bus pluckily held
The brown paper bag I puked in
And held up my hair
My motion sickness did not give her a scare!

She rose to my defence at every imagined bully
She wouldn't allow a soul, my image to sully
I blushed as she praised me loud and clear
Amrita is a trustworthy friend; she is such a dear ...

I was too young to know
I had hit the jackpot as friendships go
We had a falling out, drifted apart
We forgot to be friends,
But friendship grows kind forgiving hearts.

It conspired and brought us together again
Days of lent survived, soon forgotten.

My friend wanted to stitch me a dress
That all the cool kids were wearing
I forgot to mention, I was gawky, she
Was suave, a neat seamstress.

She measured, she tailored, she cut the cloth,
Trimmed it with lace, a pale lemon-yellow hipster
It floated sheer bliss and grace
It needed a belt and she gifted me one,
Slim sparkly silver with shiny buckles on!

Oh, my friend, thank you for the hard work, the trouble you took.
Thank you for the laughter, still gurgling like a brook,
Thank you for my new dress which still doth sashay,
In gold memoirs and annals of friendship day!

Oh, my dear! I think of you,
And even now, thirty years on
You gladden my day, and my way.

Lorraine Sicelo Mangena
ZIMBABWE

Twenty year-old Lorraine resides In Bulawayo. She is currently a first year student at the National University of Science and Technology (NUST) in Bulawayo, pursuing her bachelor's degree in Journalism and Media Studies. She is a passionate poet who has great dreams in the world of literature. Her journey of poetry has just started, and she has, so far, managed to pen down 18 poems yet to be published.
E: mathemaprince20@gmail.com
FB: @lorraine.sicelo

FRIENDS IN SOULS

Beneath the dew, laid a letter to unfold;
Behind the veil, stood my joy;
Inside a cocoon, groaned my suffocating heart;
So hidden was my soul mate.
Affection was bold in the costume of hope,
Whenever you hugged me.
Devotion was cold on the heels of pride,
For you never kissed me.
Your dizzy heart ignored my desires,
Or it was meant to provoke my seductive skills?
"wake up, that's a nightmare."

      I smiled at the dazzling love,
While we meditated the letter of friendship;
      Reality unveiled my soul mate,
When your heart beats grabbed my dreams.
Captured in romantic scenes, we garnished;
      And out of misery, we vanished.

Janelyn Dupingay Vergara
SINGAPORE / PHILIPPINES

Janelyn is from Diadi, Nueva Vizcaya, Philippines, but currently working in Singapore. Her advocacy is to promote empowerment among women and so she joined a non-profit organization called 'Uplifters', educating Domestic Workers about money management and personal growth online. She found writing a helpful tool in sending her voice of motivation to her fellow migrants through poem and essays, and is a helping hand in the activities of the Migrant Writers of Singapore. Janelyn was one of the featured speakers during the Singapore Writers Festival: 'A Labour Of Love I: Spotlight in Tagalog.' Her poem *Forgive Me* was selected for an e-book of multilingual poems by the Translating Migration. Her poem *Beauty in the Wilderness* was published in the Issue 5 of *The Tiger Moth* and is one of the story contributors in the *Call and Response 2* anthology.

E: janelynvergara24.jv@gmail.com
Facebook: @Jane Lyn Dupingay
Instagram: @jane25_lyn
YouTube: @Amazing Jane Corner

TAKE MY HAND

When you find no strength to carry on
When you feel the world has abandoned you
When the light you see starts to dim
When the loneliness becomes unbearable
When the shout of fear starts to linger
When the call of anger fills up your heart
When sanity is out of your way
When tolerance has gone nowhere
When the wound doesn't seem to heal
When the road you're on becomes confusing
When the fire within begins to vanish
When you feel exhausted of the long journey
When there's no room for you to cry
When you can't fill the empty space
When the song of joy went out of tune
Take my hand and hold on tight
Don't be afraid, I won't let go
You may not feel but I am here.

Kathleen Boyle
VIETNAM / ENGLAND

Now based in Vietnam, Kathleen Boyle (nee Dodd), was born in Liverpool, England, where she spent her childhood years before leaving to train as a teacher in Hull. Kathleen then worked as a teacher in Hull, Leeds, London and Carlisle, and at international schools in Colombia, Bahrain, Cairo, Armenia and Vietnam. She has written stories and poems throughout her life, and published a collection of poems about growing up in 1950s Liverpool entitled, *Sugar Butties and Mersey Memoirs*, as well as a collection of poems for children about a teddy bear called *Harry Pennington*. During her time in Bahrain she wrote *The Pearl House*, a short story which spans the cultural divides of Liverpool and Bahrain. While teaching in Cairo, Kathleen published her novella, *Catherine of Liverpool,* and while teaching in Vietnam, has published her recent book *The Storyteller of Cotehill Wood,* with her new book *Rosie Jones* due for publication July 2021.

E: kathdodd@aol.com

FOR MARION

Once, we sat together on a Caribbean shore,
And watched the sun set on a perfect day.
Wanderers from the North of England's
Cold and windy clime,
Toes licked by green sea,
On white sands, beneath palm trees,
Transient and magical.

Many years have passed and life has tumbled
Us down separate paths and yet no matter what,
We've kept the bond we forged back then.
We talk for hours on the phone, so much to say,
There have been times when words were not enough,
And silence would suffice, we'll always know,
That in our hearts, if life is tough
We can return to distant shores,
Where blue skies smile and sunshine rules.

It's wonderful to have a friend so wise,
Who knows life's trials are just a game,
And that reality's what lies beyond.
We rise above what pulls us down and
Stay afloat until the storm subsides,
I'll never lose my grip on life
While you are there, my friend.
There is no doubt, and ours is proof,
Some friendships never end.

Heera Nawaz
INDIA

Heera has written over 400 pieces of prose, and over 200 poems which have been published in various blogs, e-zines and anthologies globally. Her two poems *I am a Single Woman* and *Independence Day* poem have gone viral on YouTube. She has a spiritual and motivational columns in Bengaluru's main newspaper *Deccan Heral* newspaper. One of her human interest stories has been published in the Indian edition of *Reader's Digest,* and a few of her introspective stories have been published in the *Chicken Soup for the Soul*, which will shortly be made into videos. *The Times of India* has conferred Best Teacher Co-ordinator from over 2000 schools in India, and she has won Best Teacher Awards at MM Hills, and Namaste India. She was interviewed twice by *NDTV Good Times*, an Indian lifestyle channel. She has travelled extensively in India and abroad, and uses the experiences in her writing.
E: nawazheera@gmail.com

FRIENDSHIP

Friendship is a truly enervating and beautiful feeling
to explicitly show our reciprocal mutual love and care,
and how valley-deep our heartfelt emotions can be,
and how readily we are willing to mutually trust and share

Why should friendship be such a top-notch priority?
It's because friends stand by one, come what may,
friends live for us, they lie for us, and they even cry for us,
proving that "Where there's a will, there's a highway."

Due to inexplicable vicissitudes and intransigencies,
a whimsical friend can inflict indiscriminate pain,
but one should forgive the friend and one's self,
for it is only in giving and forgiving that we ultimately gain

Heart-wrenching tears are streaming down my face,
as I think of what my sacred friendship is all about,
a friend who loves me genuinely for my heart and soul,
"A friend is one who walks in when the whole world walks out"

John Tunaley
ENGLAND

John was born in Manchester in 1945. Father: foundry hand, mother; crane-driver is what his birth certificate states ... (the war was a melting pot ... throwing them together at the steel works). He now lives in Robin Hood's Bay, North Yorkshire. He's in a few writing groups ... (Natalie keeps the Whitby Library Writing Group blog up to date ... it's too tricky for John). He sticks to sonnets, as the form exercises some control of his worst excesses. They pile up ... the excesses ... He likes anthologies ... he enjoys the company ... (and there's safety in numbers ...).
E: johntunaley@yahoo.co.uk

MAGGIE AND MOLLY
(i.m.o. M & M.B)

Maggie and Molly on the sea-shore, stare
at the sea and strike natural poses ...
... gazing at distant worlds ... nebulae and
galaxies stretching to infinity,

It's not as far to Hull, but if you were
ever to break a bone badly, it might
impel you to attend its Specialist
Unit. But the cut-off Wellington would
remain behind ... a sorry reminder.

(Conscientious friends ferried her to the
Humber and exercised her puzzled dog).
Ethereal, artistic, a kind and
loving pal. Spiritual of course ... though she
had her ups and downs ... (just like the rest of us ...)

First published in *A Sonnet A Day* (2018).

Naicy Candido
SINGAPORE / PHILIPPINES

Naicy is origially from the Philippines, currently working as a domestic worker in Singapore. She has contributed to the *Call & Response 2* anthology, and is a member of the non-profit organization *Uplifters,* and a member of *Migrant Writers Singapore.*
E: Naicynew@gmail.com
FB: @Wordstring

SOUL SISTER

The womb we came;
Are not the same
Nor in separate ways
And in a different place.
She's loud I am quite
I'm here and she's there
We are a thousand miles away.

There are times
We are unable to talk
But whenever we talk
Sounds like the same olden days
The love laughs and smiles
Those memories
Are bundles with the strongest locks
For her,
I can always walk the extra miles
The heart of gold
With a beautiful soul and smile.

When she's broken
I'm here
A shoulder to cry on
An advisor nor mentor
And her pretty comfort zone.
We are not sister by blood
But we are sister by heart
Connected with a wonderful soul.
She's a beautiful creature
I've known
Hey! Soul sister!
I hope you have grown.

Melissa Nazareth
KINGDOM OF BAHRAIN

Melissa has worked on and led editorial teams for various publishing houses, and serves as Internal Liaison for the Bahrain Writers' Circle since late 2020. Her freelance works include writing for in-flight magazines and cultural websites, summarizing books, and copy editing Instagram captions (pro bono). While her niche is feature writing, she enjoys experimenting with short stories and poetry from time to time. Born and raised in Bahrain, she believes being around people of different nationalities and backgrounds taught her empathy – a virtue that has helped her as a writer. Melissa also works full-time for a non-profit organization, and part-time for her rescue cat, Mili ('found her' in Hindi), who she so named because she found her on the stairs of her building.
E: journalistmelissan@gmail.com
FB: @melissa.nazareth

YOU ARE, MY FRIEND

A cold drink on a hot summer's day,
Rainbow blossoms in the month of May,
On a dark, lonely night, a well-lit way
You are, my friend.

Wiping my tears when I cried,
Accepting my flaws with arms open wide,
The last man standing by my side
You are, my friend.

Hiding my secrets in your heart,
Sharing sweet advice, sometimes tart,
Fuelling my passion – writing – my art
You are, my friend.

Offering me a bite of what you eat,
Asking me "Mel, when will we meet?"
Being tipsy but helping me stand on my feet
You are, my friend.

Cheering for me throughout every game,
Knowing my crushes by their name,
My world without you wouldn't be the same
You know, my friend.

Michelle Morris
ENGLAND

Michelle is a South African and British writer based in Paignton, a seaside town on the coast of Tor Bay in Devon. She has been writing uplifting, inspiring and thought-provoking poetry all her life, and has been published in a number of poetry anthologies.
E: morrismichelle4@gmail.com
Twitter: @MichellePoet
Instagram: @michellemorrispoet

MY FRIEND

My friend, you are a blessing to me;
You came along and set me free;
You are always there, come rain or shine;
You know how to cheer me up when
I'm feeling down ...

My friend, I appreciate you in
All the myriad colours that you glow;
For your heart is pure and kind, and
Your compassion is always showing ...

My friend, I'll remember you
Throughout all my lifetimes,
However many there may be;
No matter how much more I
Need to learn and grow,
I was bestowed a gift with thee ...

Friendship. Always.

Marilyn Longstaff
ENGLAND

Born in Liverpool, and the daughter of Salvation Army Officers, Marilyn has spent most of her adult life in the North East of England and currently lives in Darlington. Her work has appeared in a number of magazines, anthologies and on the web, and she is currently a member of the writing, performing and publishing collective Vane Women. In 2003, Marilyn received a Northern Promise Award from New Writing North, and in 2005 gained her MA in Creative Writing from the University of Newcastle. She has written five books of poetry and, in 2011, her book *Raiment* (Smokestack Books) was selected for New Writing North's Read Regional campaign. The poems for her latest pamphlet, *The Museum of Spare Parts* (2018 Mudfog), came from her involvement in *Stemistry*, a University of Newcastle Public Engagement project, devised and run by Lisa Matthews, to consider creative responses to modern genomics. Her other books are: *Puritan Games* (Vane Women Press, 2001), *Sitting Among The Hoppers* (Arrowhead Press, 2004) and *Articles of War* (Smokestack Books, 2017).
E: marilynclong@aol.com

ON NOT DIVING INTO THE WRECK

In Whitby on the last day of April
standing on West Pier, gazing
into high-tide-green waters

she felt compelled to jump
although she knew even in
the heat of the day, this sea

was freezing, and that the currents
at the harbour mouth were worse than
treacherous.   She had a notion

that she would sink straight down, and yet
would still be able to see and breathe
as normal.   Needless to say

she didn't do it. Common sense
(where would she leave her handbag?)
and fear prevailed.   Instead

she sat basking in unexpected sun.
When she got home, she read
that poem by Adrienne Rich

about going down, down, down
facing her demons and the wreckage
which she herself had never done

although driving to see her friend Joanna
she had such good words in her head
good enough to release all that pain and anger.

Why didn't she write them down?

Máire Malone
ENGLAND / REPUBLIC OF IRELAND

Máire was born and reared in Dublin where she worked as a medical secretary. She moved to the UK, studied Arts and Psychology and followed a career in Counselling & Psychotherapy. Several of her poems have been selected and published by Ver Poets, and other anthologies. She has had short story prize wins in *Scribble* magazine. A story was shortlisted in Words and Women Competition, 2018. She was selected for a place on the Novel Studio Course in 2017 where she completed a draft of her debut novel, *The Dream Circle*. Her novel has been selected as a Finalist in Eyelands International Book Awards 2019, and *The Irish Echo*, New York, published an essay about it earlier this year.
E: maireowens@aol.com
W: www.mairemalone.com

IN MEMORY OF A GOOD FRIEND (DIED 1995)

Very dark and very kind
The first to say come for a coffee and mean it
When I felt so strange and raw in Glasgow
You baked fresh scones and gave me games and toys
My boys have outgrown them you said
And when we moved house you lent us curtains for a while
Oh, and a little wooden desk with initials carved all over
Now we've outgrown that and passed it on.
You took us under your wing
Now angels have carried you away
You stood at my kitchen sink and said
They think it's cancer
We cried a bit then spoke about your boys
I watched you fade away and lied
You look so well
You went downhill very quickly in the end
Your funeral was beautiful
How strange to see your mother so like you
Your sister said you shed no tears before you died
You saved your strength for your husband and your boys.

Shagun Shukla
INDIA

Living in Vishakhapatnam in the peninsular southern part of India, Shagun is an intuitive Reiki practitioner who believes there's something good in every individual or situation. Her first book *Altitudinis – Seekers, Sinners & Secrets* is a collaborative scientific, romantic thriller written as a fluid, cohesive story by ten Indian writers. A contributor to an anthology for women's issues, published by the eminent International Human Rights Art Festival (IHRAF), her poems are also published on a global platform in *Active Muse*, a prestigious online journal of literature, poetry, and art. A lifelong learner, her scientific temperament comes from her post graduate degree in Microbiology, an MBA with specialization in HR, along with a Bachelor in Education degree. A mom, homemaker, friend, writer with her heart in the mind spot, she believes in the power of thoughts.

E: shagunshukla@gmail.com
W: www.writingsofshagun.wordpress.com

FRAGRANT FRIENDSHIPS

From the cradle we grew together
Your dimpled smiles and my reckless laughter
Our frolicking in muddy grasslands of school
Climbing trees or chasing butterflies unseen
Studying together, our scores never mattered
All that was held dear then, was our mammoth plans
Of succeeding in the days that will come later in life
The richly fragrant biryani cooked to perfection
Is how our friendship grows till now
We, the dainty girls ... were out to change the old world

Somewhere on the road to grow, I let be
My dreams asleep and my heart stifle a beat
As I raised a family of three, I simple forgot ... to be!
You found the person hidden within
Cleaned and reignited the passions of living
My dreams flowed from my home to the streets
A camera, coffee flask and the older yet wiser me
Chased the stories cast in stones so old and rare
Life changed; it blossomed when I met you
Fragrant like a lone jasmine unfurling in the morning air

On those lanes one fine day
From another life, I met you, my friend
Your unabashed zest for happiness flew me away
Like a timeless beauty, nuggets of wisdom you shared deep
Your simple joy in sipping tea while sitting under the trees
Matched mine and our moments together recharged my soul
Like petrichor, it fills my lungs and keeps me sane in turbulent times
Till date the fragrance holds dear though the old trees are not there
anymore

As the leaves of life turned yellow
Another dream wriggled to take shape that lay dormant before
When others my age were getting ready to hang in their boots
I picked up my pen to write my anecdotes
My life's funny yet crazy moments
The imperfectly happy or sometimes gloomy days
I let my thoughts flow into words written in ink
Because somewhere down this path
On a temple lane, our minds collided
And you believed in me

The incense fragrance mixed with my chelpark ink
Inching me further towards my dream

Every friendship is special
Teaching life a living lesson
Yet this one steers to heart the closest
All through these years, at life's every twist and turn
Whenever I look back, I see a pair of gentle brown eyes
And a comforting chest to bury my head deep within
My life partner, my best buddy, your love guides me every moment
Not just to live but to dream a life worth loving and living
Like richly brewed coffee ... your aroma fills with hope my very being

Ergasheva Mashhura
UZBEKISTAN

From Samarkand region of the Republic of Uzbekistan, Ergasheva is a poet and a student at the Samarkand State of University,Faculty of Philology. Her poems have been published *The Poet's Journal, Dilimiz and Edebiyatimiz,* and others.
E: mashhuraergasheva95@gmail.com

A LETTER TO MY FRIEND

My friend!
The life of our dream is prolonged.
The longing for our lives has been
so many guests
if we get tired of them.
The barren times that embraced us.
Our crippled chests burned, burned, crushed.
We sold ourselves to broker of Love
and caught, to itself - to God!

Prof. Jeton Kelmendi

KOSOVO / BELGIUM

Prof. Jeton Kelmendi received his Bachelor of Arts in Mass communication from the University of Pristina, and completed his post-graduate studies at the Free University of Brussels, Belgium, specializing in International and Security Studies, where he finished his second master degree in Diplomacy. Jeton did a PhD in The Influence of media in EU Political Security Issues, and is a professor at AAB University College, Kosovo. He has written poetry, prose, essays and short stories for many years, and is a regular contributor to a number of publications across the region. He made his name in Kosovo after the publication of his first book The Century of Promises (Shekulli i Premtimeve) in 1999, and has published a number of books since. His poems have been translated into thirty-seven languages, and published widely. Jeton has won a large number of awards for his work, and is a member of many international arts and cultural institutions and clubs. According to a number of eminent literary critics, Jeton is a genuine representative of modern Albanian poetry.

E: jetonkelmendi@gmail.com
W: www.jetonkelmendi.page.tl
FB: @jeton.kelmendi1

FRIENDSHIP IN THE PANDEMIC TIME

I.

Only myself accompanies me
took the place of all the friends
all dear friends

and now only myself believes me
when I approach
all my people start
with numbers
in fact some with letters in the messenger
it's because they keep me away,
away I keep them too
you sir,
you are the only one who does not scare me
nor does it frighten you
Mr myself.

II.

The days we spend closed,
without any exit
only thoughts and a few words come out
around the meaning

daily I climbed to the top of
memory
at night I go down to myself
time sits there in its own bed
how to wake it up
or even time is scaring from
pandemic COVID19.

III.

Today's life on the frame
of tomorrow
when love does not dare to love
properly
so is this Pandemic to us

and sloppy imagination

from pleasure endowed with dilemmas
extinguished almost without occurrence
what if someone
that I have dreamed, to seek me
something more,
am I the one who transcended time
or time is running out
in me ...

Kathleen Bleakley
AUSTRALIA

Kathleen lives in Wollongong, on the south coast of eastern Australia. She has five published poetry & prose collections: *Letters,* (a Pocket Poet, 2020), *Azure* (a Pocket Poet, 2017), *Lightseekers,* photography by 'pling (2015), *jumping out of cars*, with Andrea Gawthorne, images by 'pling, (2004), and *Passionfruit & Other Pieces*, with prints by Hannah Parker (1995). Kathleen's poetry has been widely published in literary journals, including internationally.
E: kathleen@pling.id.au

AEROGRAMS

Dear Arthur
we wrote aerograms
both loved to cover paper & envelope
tiny writing, you & I, packed with adventures

we wrote aerograms
between northern and southern hemispheres
tiny writing, you & I, packed with adventures
your Barossa Valley bike rides

between northern and southern hemispheres
past vineyards with russet and claret leaves
your Barossa Valley bike rides
my Swedish lakes

past vineyards with russet and claret leaves
you stopped to sample a few
my Swedish lakes, vast as oceans
forests of birch and oaks

you stopped to sample a few
burgundies, Rieslings and sauternes
forests of birch and oaks, I walked
longest, lightest summer nights

burgundies, rieslings and sauternes
you filled the cellar for my return
longest, lightest summer nights
then home to winter, firelit

you filled the cellar for my return
wrote one last aerogram then I was home to winter
firelit, your words flowing
Dear Arthur, my dad and friend

First published in *Letters*, Ginninderra Press, 2020.

Amelia Fielden
AUSTRALIA

Amelia lives in Wollongong on Australia's south-east coast. She is a keen poet who writes mainly in traditional Japanese poetic forms such as tanka and tanka tales. Amelia's ninth collection *More Farewells* is scheduled for publication in December 2021.
E: anafielden@gmail.com

"ROUND UP THE USUAL SUSPECTS"*

Pre-Christmas lunch gathering 2020.
The end of a calamitous pandemic year. None of us infected by covid-19.
But there have been losses: two husbands, a son, a grandson.
Cancers. Surgeries. Exacerbation of chronic illnesses.
Yet thirteen from the class of '58 have made it here. All in manageable
health, and positive spirits. On the verandah of a village restaurant we toast
the safe arrival of a first great-granddaughter.

> old roses climb
> clinging to the trellises ...
> round our table
> school girl voices tell stories
> of their generations

* An iconic utterance in the film *Casablanca*, released in 1942, the birth year of most of my school friends.

Nivedita Karthik

INDIA

Nivedita is a graduate in Immunology from the University of Oxford. She is an accomplished Bharatanatyam dancer and published poet. She also loves writing stories. Her poetry has appeared in *Glomag, The Society of Classical Poets, The Epoch Times, The Bamboo Hut, Eskimopie, The Sequoyah Cherokee River Journal, The Ekphrastic Review,* and *Visual Verse*. Nivedita also regularly contributes to the open mics organized by Rattle Poetry. She currently resides in Gurgaon, and works as a scientific and medical editor/reviewer.
E: nivedita5.karthik@gmail.com
W: www. justrandomwithnk.com
YouTube: @JustrandomwithNK

WHAT A TRUE FRIEND DOES

When dusk falls and the moon is hidden
and darkness shadows your eyes,
know that memories of us will come unbidden
into your mind, lighting it up like a million fireflies.

When your pupils drown in saltwater,
sinking quickly under the weight of your veiny, marbled heart,
I will be your personal breakwater
and give you my shoulder so you can rise again and restart.

DEAR FRIEND, I WISH YOU WERE HERE

Today I read a book
a book on an astronaut lost in space
in a post-apocalyptic world.

Today I saw a movie
a movie about a man stranded
on a desert island.

Then, I picked up the phone
the phone so I could connect with you
you on the other side of the globe.
        But you were not there …

So I took a jug of water
a jug of water to green the plants
the plants that stand so still and stoic
        Nary a breeze ruffling their leaves.

The silence, it gets to me.

Without hearing your voice,
I am lost in space
My mental space
I am stranded
        Stranded in a sea of my own thoughts
I am parched
        Parched of your infectious smile.

Anamika Nandy
INDIA

Anamika hails from Digboi, Assam. By profession she is an educationist. She loves to write poems and to express her emotions in words, and enjoys working towards the development of a better society.
E: anamika.sweety1431@gmail.com

A BLESSED BOND

From the seventh heaven,
Comes down this blessed bond.
Drop by drop it builds its entity,
Among the fair souls.

Like sprightly sunshine,
Cheers in every step.
Like soothing moonbeams,
Embalms the sporadic subdued bosom.
Roots to fruits it sticks,
For a second it never flicks.
The cord of loyalty strongly binds,
Gender biasness it never decides.

Never lets one down,
Never leaves one alone.
Bridging all gaps in life,
A tower of strength it stands tight,
Where love and understanding glows bright,
Bitterness elopes from this sacred room,
Solidarity comes to reign supreme.
Haloed is this true bond,
The name is 'blessed friendship bond'.

Suranjit Gain
BANGLADESH

Recognized by a large number of international literary festivals, Suranjit is a national and international awarded poet. He has published around ninety books in Bengali, Hindi and English, in several countries worldwide.
E: suranjitgain300@gmail.com

DIGNITY OF FRIENDSHIP

Every one should preserve
the dignity of friendship.
It is a little word
but immense signification.
All should contemplate
about the importance of alliance.
Friendship is really
a sacred bond.
It's a great obligation;
should carry out towards friend.
To hold down
the respect of kinship
we have to be
the companion
in grief and pleasure
for ever.
Above all in life
and death.

Ailenemae Salvador
HONG KONG / PHILIPPINES

Ailenemae has had two of her poems included in the *The Tiger Moth review eco journal photos issue #5 (*Jan.2021), one poem included in an anthology entitled *Dancing With Death (*April 2021), and three poems in the anthology *Diversity: A Poetry Collection: on peace, love, and empathy*. She published her first book in March, 2021 titled Beyond the Sunset.
E: ailenemaesalvador051184@gmail.com

MY LIFE SAVER

When I am having a bad day,
Your smile could go a long way.
Please make sure to put one on,
And keep it until the day is gone.

You are like a star that twinkles and glows,
You are like the ocean that gently flows.
You are like gold that should be treasure,
You are in my heart that is for sure.

You are my angel, always there to guide my path,
Someone I can trust until the moment of my death.
You save me from the darkness I belong,
Which I stayed for quite so long.

When you love and hold me without any fear,
Happiness spreads throughout the atmosphere.
You look to me with grace and confidence,
You and I talk about all joyful things without any rants.

You might not know what this deed,
That can be done for a friend in need.
It might save me from any kind of pain,
Of a sadness, which I cannot contain.

Don't ask me, what a smile can do,
Because I'm sure it once helped me and you.
In your camaraderie, the good times move very fast.
I swear I'll cherish you after my own life will last.

Jennifer Sisasenkosi Chiveya
ZIMBABWE

Jennifer is 24 years of age and a poet, writer and activist based in Bulawayo. Her artwork and poetry is inspired by the need to see change in social, economical and political spaces. The ultimate goal to be the change she wants to see in her community in creating a safe and conducive society for this generation, and the one to come. Her words ought to speak and advocate for those who can not do so themselves, and act as an escape and therapeutic window from the world.

E: @chiveyajennifer@gmail.com
FB: @Jennifer S Chiveya
Instagram: @jenn_cheev
Twitter: @ChiveyaJennifer

DECEASED MUSE

It all crumbled down in vain,
Our adventures went down the drain.
We were supposed to grow older together,
Keep going and hustling,
Never let the fire burn down.

Days are darker now,
Without your smile,
And your contagious laugh.
Nights are even longer now,
The stars are dim,
They don't shine the same anymore.

I miss your presence.
All I do is hold on to our memories,
Cherish the moments we shared,
And laugh at our old jokes.
In my heart you will always exist,
Because legends never die,
They forever live on.

Manju Kanchuli Tiwari
NEPAL

Manju is a poet, fiction writer, playwright, essayist and freelance writer. With over 15 books already published, she is a life-member of Nepal Academy, and a retired assistant professor of clinical psychology and English literature. She has delivered her literary performances in different parts of the world, and received many National and International Awards including the International Writer's award. She had presented a solo poetry exhibition in Beijing, and contributed literary works both in Nepali and English languages.

E: manjukanchuli@yahoo.com
W: www.uiowa.edu/iwp

DISTANCE

Presences are isolated
Parallel movement of feet on the green carpet
The gestures! Simultaneously, so active
Such an attempt to ...

How better were it the early morning
Of those days
No accident would have marked me
No injury and distortion of the arms!

This very moment evening tea in hand
Lips that sip, eyes that gaze
An occasional smile
A few inches of distance
Doors surround us: closed, open, half open, half closed
Supper at 10pm, on dingy lit table cloth
Of two different oblong tables
In separate buildings
Miles distance

The next morning skulls meet
And hands convey in gestures concave and vexed!
The corpus – coliseums':"Good morning!" voice
Hearts and heave of hearts — call them 'colleagues'
Then these joined hemispheres set apart

TIGER IN THE CITY

Sparkles the music as emerald
Concealed in a green bush
In its midst the ditch reveals a thin green snake
No poison in its fang
Its eggs in water beautiful to look at
Splendid like pearl's teeth, like heart beat!
Before I could praise it, I was in sleep' deep cage
At the moment a tiger bellowed in the city
His voice as big as whale's egg, I imagine
His emerald-eyes as green as mountain trees
I woke up and thank a silk worm
Survived unharmed in the pages on my shelf
I mellowed its song into my own blanket and quilt
The tiger's heart beats weigh
With emerald beads
With snake's eggs
And with lightning eyes
The eyes bellow warm light into the dark glass of evening
A man in his hand a torch-glows, in the city every night
Ever since their converged dazzling lightning borders them
That frightens the tiger and scares the man

AN OLD WOMAN

An old woman peeps through her window
Democracy in her yard
Resting under her chin
Her own beautiful wrinkled hand
A wonderful formless form in peacefulness
Chiselling it to boost the aroma of the goddess
In her nose, eyes, mouth and ears
Endurance in rumple, glory in ironed crumple
Tolerance in reticence, concrete
Is it suffering? Is it bliss?
Unknown!
One cannot see
It is smeared inside the stone-wall of her face
Her vocal cord is shut or perhaps cut long before
She looks beautiful; a beautiful bust of gallantry
A tourist takes its pictures from various angles
Made of stone!
Perhaps a goddess in the city of the temples
A bestowed honour to lie shut
So suffocating wind into the fore-wall!
Is it for ever?

Elisabetta Bagli
SPAIN / ITALY

Elisabetta was born in Rome (Italy), and she has lived in Madrid (Spain) since 2002. She has a degree in Economics and Business from La Sapienza in Rome, and writes poetry, short stories and essays. She is also a translator and interpreter of Spanish. She is the author of several poetry books, a compilation of stories, a children's book, and articles and essays for newspapers and digital magazines around the world, and her poems and writings have been translated into thirteen languages. Operating in more than a hundred national and international anthologies, Elisabetta is the President and a Former member of the Jury in many national and international literary prizes. She has collaborated with the Esther Koplowitz Foundation, based in Madrid (Spain), and has received many prestigious awards, including the Mayte Spínola Diploma of Honour for artistic merit from the Pro Arte y Cultura group in 2017 (Spain), the Distinction for Outstanding Woman in culture, 2019 awarded by the Latin American Women's Forum, Mar del Plata (Argentina), the Italian Award for Culture 2019 awarded by the Italian Ambassador Stefano Sannino in Madrid (Spain), Najiman Prize in Lebanon on July 2020 and many others prizes in Italy, in Spain and all over the world for cultural merits.
E: elibagli7@gmail.com
W: www.elisabettabagli.com

HANDS

A new feeling,
Hands in the night
And fingers glistening,
Clutching the future
Of cross-cutting destinies.

Vivid hands desiring one another,
Unsuspecting eyes smiling
At the new life,
Seeking comfort,
Unfolding in the world.

The groove of each sorrow
Is in the wrinkles of the skin
Announcing
The abandonment of hands
That support each other
Beyond eternity.

I HAVE SEEN THE SPRING COME

I find myself in this silent cage
Made of brick and glass,
Longing for another silence,
That of nature,
In which I perceived
The pleasant sounds
Of our Mother Earth,
In which my life
Stopped in infinite moments
And my thoughts were thickening,
Meditating on pain
On the passage of time
And the impossibility of living it all.

I've seen spring come
From this cage,
The sunlight change intensity,
The colours shine again
In the few trees
That inhabit my street,
The vivid reflections of the flowers
In the neighbour's windowsill,
The same whom every night
I see applauding our heroes
Struggling to stop
This wind that seems to be telling us:
"You are no longer necessary!"

I've seen spring come
And its memories, the storms
And the smell of wet earth,
Memories of melancholy,
Of screaming at the Sky
Which does not refuse the drops
That once sailed across my being
And now they are still falling
But only on thirsty pastures and meadows,
Washing eternal forests,
Cleaning the whole world,
Forgetting that I'm withering
In a prison without bars.

You are so vast and free,
Mother of all Mothers
And I think of you who saw my birth,
Who taught me to feel,
Waking my heart from the dark,
Whispering pure words to my soul
Pure like your beauty from which living water flows,
From which flourishes the unmatched strength
Of your harmony, a source of inspiration
For every human being,
The sap that nourishes and saves
And that now hides from our eyes
That are full of hope to live in you again.

Ankita Patel
INDIA

Ankika resides in Mumbai, and is a US citizen. It's been a time of revival of passion for her; as a scientist her actions are left-brain dominated, so she has taken this opportunity to metamorphize, and activate and enhance her right-brain by indulging in some writing. It has been a therapeutic journey so far, and making her life a rather balanced chemical equation.
E: ankita@alumni.stanford.edu

SCHOOL DAYS

"Those were the days"
Often I find my mind retrace
As my thoughts graze
to a past of purer pasture ...

From the nappy days
to the sleepover stays
Those fun annual plays
Childhood crushes and craze
Navigating the life maze
For a bright future, eyes ablaze

The scorching heat of the blazing sun
The piercing eyes of the teachers
Oh, so stern ...
The chitter chatter as we cycled to school
Our callow ways of acting and looking cool

Our famous rickshaw-wala and gang
Cramping 10 of us into his three-sitter caravan
We joked, we played, we teased, we sang
Rushing running into classes as the bell rang

Those school bags, heavier than us
Ah! the perfect tie, all the fuss
Playing volleyball, dodgeball
Campaigning for the CR elections
The voting count, the final call

Fridays in the assembly square
Standing height order with flare ...
Chanting the school prayer
Ready for the Principal's blare

The super fun lunch breaks,
The tiffin sharing,
Over snacks, lunches and cakes
The teasing and silly couple pairing ...

The SUPW spirit calling
the knitting, the sewing, thread works
A class of intermingling

the meek, the charmers, the bullies
the geeks and the dorks

Our educational school trips
Best memories, lifelong friendships
We gossiped, we mingled, fell asleep
Our face plastered
with lipstick and toothpaste heaps ...
The antakshari on overnight bus rides,
Ghost stories, pulling legs and taking sides ...

Our class, one tightly knit brood
Divided in views, united we stood
Our families familiar with everyone
Together, we all shone brighter than the sun ...

Times of naïve nicety
airhead altercations
disputes and debates
imbecile imputations ...
Oh, those were the times ...

Diaspora
As we grew
We grew apart
Walked away
On different branches of life
Held strongly together by
the stem
Of our growing years
Paths led around the world
But we all stay deep rooted
To our alma matter
Prakash Higher Secondary School

A SPACE I CALL MINE

As I set eyes upon the vastness of the grassland,
My body aches for the softness of my mother's hand

My mind races back to the space I call mine
Just thoughts of her sending chills down my spine

The infinite expanse in my mother's heart
Which has held me high from the very start

A bottomless pit of love,
we walk as one, hand in glove

A space so pious, with a special sweet bias
A space with no judgements, full of adjustments

A love with no condition, navigating me through each transition
No fret, no favor, through every problem, my life saver

As I grow old and bold, wind under my wings
With a heavy heart, goodbye she sings
And a nest for me, she sobs and strings

And I return to the nest, after a world-wide quest
Of dreams and dejections
Desires and deceptions
Exhilarations and agitations
Love and loss
Everything gone for a toss
Success turning to failure
Despair with no cure
I return to my space
My mother's heart, my base

The space out there merging with the space within ...
Where do you end and where do I begin?

Ndaba Sibanda
ZIMBABWE / ETHIOPIA

Originally from Bulawayo, Zimbabwe but now living in Addis Ababa, Ethiopia, Ndaba is the author of *Notes, Themes, Things And Other Things, The Gushungo Way, Sleeping Rivers, Love O'clock, The Dead Must Be Sobbing, Football of Fools, Cutting-edge Cache, Of the Saliva and the Tongue, When Inspiration Sings In Silence, The Way Forward, Sometimes Seasons Come With Unseasonal Harvests, As If They Minded:The Loudness Of Whispers, This Cannot Be Happening :Speaking Truth To Power, The Dangers Of Child Marriages:Billions Of Dollars Lost In Earnings And Human Capital, The Ndaba Jamela and Collections* and *Poetry Pharmacy*. Ndaba's work has received Pushcart Prize and Best of the Net nominations. Some of his work has been translated into Serbian.
E: loveoclockn@gmail.com

NETWORK FRIENDSHIPS AND HARDSHIPS

Excitement welled up in her heart
Sweet dream after sweet dream
She dreamt and drummed about it
All by virtue of a mere friend request
On a media network, an invitation
Extended by a man who, in earnest
Was looking for business partners
However she took the request too far -
As an unspoken marriage proposal!
When her assertions reached the man
He didn't take kindly to such claims
He did an instantaneous deed indeed
Had she stepped on the tail of a lion?
Because the slim man had no gentility
To find out more about her wild claims
He simply unfriended her on the spot!

Rozalia Aleksandrova
BULGARIA

Rozalia was born in the magical Rhodope Mountains, the cradle of Orpheus, and now lives in Plovdiv, one of Europe's oldest settlements. She is the author of 11 poetry books: *The House of My Soul* (2000), *Shining Body* (2003), *The Mystery of the Road* (2005), *The Eyes of the Wind* (2007), *Parable of the key* (2008), *The Conversation between Pigeons* (2010), *Sacral* (2013), *The Real Life of Feelings* (2015), *Pomegranate from Narrow* (2016), *Brushy* (2017), and *Everything I did not say* (2019). Editor and compiler of over ten literary almanacs, collections and anthologies, she is a member of the Union of Bulgarian Writers. In March 2006 she created a poetic-intellectual association Quantum and Friends for the promotion of quantum poetry in civil society. She is initiator and organizer of the International Festival of Poetry 'Spirituality Without Borders' from 2015, which, for seven consecutive years, has brought together poets from Bulgaria, Europe and the world in an atmosphere of tolerance, friendship and the love of human speech. Every year the Festival publishes a poetry almanac, with which the participating poets present themselves to the Plovdiv and foreign audiences. The Festival also participates in joint initiatives with other festivals in Bulgaria and abroad including 'Festiwal poezji slowianskiej' (London), 'Festiwal poezji slowianskiej' (Czechowice-Dziedzice, Polska), 'Festival of Poetry' (Turkey), and others, and in Plovdiv: the International Festival Days of Thracian Culture.
E: rozalia54@yahoo.com
FB: @РозалияАлександрова

POEM 1

This is how you understand silence -
dragged from the dunes.
A beautiful shadow of a friend.
Fallen silent next to the strings.
And a wind of ancient waves
enchants horizons.
The sailors of the third dimension
dream of divine bets.

POEM 2

You're alive, my friend!
No more postponing.
Alive! And it's you again.
The wind will stretch hopes again.
A rescued love is screaming.
God's will - sun.
And abyss.
Earthly-heavenly oars.
You are a guardian
of eternal youth.
And you are winning over fear.

Daniela Marian
ROMANIA

Daniela is a prolific writer and poet who has, so far, written over 500 poems. She is a graduate of the University Mihail Kogalniceanu in the Faculty of Law - specialization in Legal Sciences, with a postgraduate course in Medical Information Management and Biostatistics at the Grigore T. Popa University of Medicine and Pharmacy, in Iași. She has published poems in several anthologies and magazines, both in her country and worldwide, includin: *Anthology of Literature and Contemporary Art, Take and Write, The Writer, Evening Star, Cultural Harmonies,* and many others. She was also awarded the Diploma of Excellence for the Promotion of Romanian Culture and Spirit in the Centennial Year in the Living Flame of Our Great Union (1918-2018).
E: dmariania3@gmail.com

LOVE FLED

On the path that leads to the spring
I came across many thorns and weeds
She had long been cared for by a muse
She is wearing colourful velvet dresses
The firs greeted her with admiration
They were towering, they were proud
The blackberries were scattered in lace
The fruit turned black
A pair of deer were coming
they smelled of intoxicating perfume

The days of the past were running fast
They seemed to compete with love
A love from the abode of my heart
It's never been since
It was as if seven lives had passed
Mankind does not change its habits
The same thing has been going on for centuries
Whole floors of deforested forests stretch
Are there seedlings in nurseries?
Who is volunteering with them?
The bride and groom are in no hurry
They will have a fairytale wedding
Spring, summer or sometime
Old age is not a respite, it does not wait
Her hair hurriedly puts on her white coat
He put on his glasses to see the wrinkles
Now it's a shame
I do not tend to break this new habit
Everything is upside down
Poets hold the pen in their hands
Who listens to them? they are tired of writing
I put melodramas on white paper
Compare it to the snow cape
The seasons don't listen to them either
Or mixed up in short words
When in insistent words of love
Love hid in an angel of the soul put his purple wave crucified on the altar of Jesus.

Madhavi Tiwary

KINGDOM OF BAHRAIN / INDIA

Madhavi's first rendezvous with writing was at college where her scribblings - which she fondly called 'poems' - were proudly and regularly passed on to like-minded class mates. It then took a decade for her to pick up writing again with zeal and zest. As a result, in the past few years, she has written about fifty articles and editorial columns, and has written as many poems, many of which are still hatching in the warmth of her private closet.

E: madhavi.dwivedi@gmail.com

FRIENDSHIP – A NEW DIMENSION

Is he my friend –
that bundle of bones
crouching in that far off corner?
Or the girl knifing my heart
with her full eyes and
empty stomach?
Or that bearded man
curling over a searing stone
breaking his whole day's fast
with a half rotten banana in one hand
and a quarter full water bottle in the other?
Maybe that woman
leaning against a drying tree
trying to somehow hold in place
her bulging belly?
Or the old man
hesitating even to perch on a roadside bench
lest he dirties it with
the remnants of his rags?

Could I ever be their friend?
What if I extended my hand to
the lonely man in the far off corner?
What if I shared my Belgium chocolate bar
with that bundle of bones?
What if I offered the bearded man
a seat in a room swarming with all those
fragile French cut glass curios?
What if I put a hand underneath
the spasming belly?
What if I sat beside the old man
and put my arm round his
drooping defeated shoulders?

Will then a connection fall in place,
although our paths may not cross again?
Will they remember me fondly?
Will they want to chance on me again?
Will their heart sometimes beat for me?

I guess, yes, we will be friends ...

Mónika Tóth
ROMANIA

Mónika graduated high-school in Humanities at Körösi Csoma Sándor in Covasna, and then studied accountancy. She is interested in culture, reading, painting, philosophy and photography, and enjoys Romanian, Turkish, Russian, South-American and Norwegian literature. Passionate about poetry, her new book *Your absence makes me thin* (*Soványít hiányod*) has just been released.
E: monikatoth314@yahoo.com

YOUR FRIENDSHIP
Dedicate my nice Romanian friend V.D.

Your friendship
Gentle as breeze
Your friendship
Sweet as sugar
Your friendship
Enchanting as music
I adore your friendship

Maria Nemy Lou Rocio
HONG KONG / PHILIPPINES

Maria is from the Philippines and currently working in Hong Kong. She started to write poetry when she was in High School, but only found her way back into writing three years ago, when she started to work abroad. She expresses her thoughts and emotions through writing poetry and short stories, and as a way of overcoming the trials of being separated from her family. She is an active member of 'Arts in Me', a writing platform in Singapore founded by The Migrant Writers of Singapore, and is a team-leader of Uplifters, a non-profit, non-government organization in Hong Kong that gives free online money management courses.

E: misnemz@gmail.com
FB: @Marias-Corner-My-Poem-My-Story-103973511564918

CONNECTION

Friends come,
In different ways
From a table,
for two
Or from a bench,
At the park
A glass of water,
Or from
a piece of biscuit.

My friends?
They come from
the drop
of an ink
Our curlicues
Entangle
Our words
Rhyme perfectly.

We understand
Each other
If one
needs a space, we
pause
We respect,
each other
Piece
By piece.

So for as long as
Poetry lives
Our friendship,
Lives
Our connection
Is our
Masterpiece.

ODE TO JANE LYN

I was wandering,
distracted by my thoughts, and
confined deeply in my emotions.
Looking for someone with a pure heart,
for someone who will listen,
to my unspoken fears of rejection,
someone who will feel,
my relentless predicaments.

I found her in my deepest sorrow,
when my mind was giving up,
and my heart was being crushed.
She touched me with her words,
lifting my soul,
giving new life to my spirits.

With my broken wings,
she did not mend,
instead she gave me her own,
so that I can fly again,
to see the beauty in everything,
while making me believe I belong there.

With a pure heart,
that's always ready to care for others
without asking in return,
a selfless damsel, giving so much love,
in this world of pretensions and disgust,
beneath the draperies she hides,
reflecting nothing but her visible silhouette.

As I soar now within the clouds,
the gentle wind that blows beneath my wings,
pushing me up every time I drift,
guiding me as others come to join me
wishing that someday I will lead the flock.
with no reservations,
to a place where they should be.

Her smile I will forever keep,
it makes my heart glow,
and her eyes that looks at everyone,

with radiating compassion
I will always admire,
and her heart, overflowing with love,
and embracing others.
I wish to stay there, whatever matters,
to be held and kept,
and be with her fruitful wanderlust
... forever

Audrey Savage
ENGLAND

Audrey is one hundred years-old, and lives in Kent. She is very new to poetry writing, and this is only her second contribution.
E: savageae@hotmail.com

FRIENDSHIP

Friendship without a doubt
Is something one can't do without
It comes in all sorts of ways
Unexpectedly on some days

As you grow older or you move
Different people you get to meet
Writing is not for everyone
It's considered a chore by some

In an emergency
If needs be
They drop everything
To see to thee.

When transport once
Had failed to come
And taxis were
On the school run

I called my friend out of bed
She took me to hospital instead
Goodness knows what I'd have done
Had she not been able to come

She has now moved
And lives far away
I miss her visits
From day to day.

We keep in touch
But it's not the same
As having her near
When she always came.

Barbara Webb
ENGLAND

Barbara lives in Kent, which is where she retired to some while ago. She is very new to poetry, having only started writing within the past few months.
E: barbarawebb278@gmail.com

THE FRIENDS THAT WE FIND

Throughout life we make many friends
They enrich the lives that we lead
When desperate for some company
They will be there for us when in need

When times become a struggle
And you require a friendly ear
There is always someone to turn to
Someone who you hold very dear

As time passes over a number of years
Just like the ebb and flow of the sea
Some flit in and out of our lives
While others are with us eternally

Of course, it's a two-way thing
Be a giver as well as a taker
A partnership that has to work
To reap the benefits of your labour

The friends that are there throughout
Who have shared the light and the dark
Will have the greatest understanding and
Always be there with a kindly remark

Enjoy your friends while you can
As they might not always be about
Let them know how much they mean
With a gesture that puts it in no doubt

This fairground of life with its tos and fros
Ups and downs and merry-go-rounds
How much harder it would be if we were
Without the friends that we found

YOU

When life is a challenge
You are always there
Knowing just what to do and
Making things easier to bear

Without you by my side
I would be unable to cope
You find the right words to use
And give me so much hope

It isn't just what you say
You listen and nod and bring
The comfort that is needed
To release the pain within

You always seem to know how
To make things easier for me
Your selfless love is moving
Your welcome arms set me free

You make everything seem better
And you just seem to find a way
Of raising up my spirits and
Helping me through each day

If a time comes you are not there
I would be half the person I am
I would have to find another way
And I'm not sure that I can

Barbra Dean
SPAIN / ENGLAND

Barbra's first jobs were in public relations and advertising. Then she joined *SHE* magazine as Assistant Fashion Editor arranging photography and fashion shows. She also freelanced for many magazines and newspapers. Later on she worked for a well-known agony aunt, and was responsible for answering her mail. She has also been a film extra appearing in many soaps for television, a lot of the time spent in the pub background pretending to drink! As a mature student in her fifties she successfully completed a degree in Humanities, and her subjects were English, Psychology and Computing. She also did Drama, which she loved, and appeared in a few productions. She has written a children's book *The Multicoloured Hat*, which has been translated into Spanish called *El Sombrero Multicolor,* and is suitable for adults too who are learning either language.
E: babsiedean@gmail.com

TO A VERY DEAR FRIEND

To a very dear friend, is this really the end
Are you leaving without a goodbye
It just seems so cruel, you've no time at all
Your family and friends asking why
You've lived life to the full, and seen it all
You've travelled and done all you can
You're a wonderful wife, were so full of life
A fabulous mother and gran
You're too young to go, you don't want to we know
Why has this happened to you
To go through this nightmare, you must be needed up there
But you're wanted on this planet too
So just before, you walk out of the door
And close it behind you for good
We send a white dove, who carries our love
And if we could change things we would
So through all the tears, we'll remember the years
Of laughter and sharing together
You've been a great friend, we don't want it to end
But you'll live in our hearts forever

Dr. Sarah Clarke
KINGDOM OF BAHRAIN

Sarah is from the UK and has lived in the Middle East since 2006. Her poems have featured in three anthologies of *The Poet Magazine, Suicide, Lockdown 2020* and *A New World*. She is also the Principal Writer for the travel series *101 Things to See and Do*. Sarah is the Founder of the Baloo's Buddies in Bahrain - a non-profit program using pet dogs to enhance the life and social skills of children of all abilities with communication difficulties. When not working on large scale inclusive projects, Sarah enjoys writing in a variety of formats including children's literature and poetry. Writing primarily on themes of inclusion, mental health and the environment, Sarah's poems and artwork has been featured in a number of poetry events and exhibitions in Bahrain since 2018.

E: sarah@dscwll.com
FB: @Baloosbuddies
FB: @@sarahclarke888

JUST LIKE YESTERDAY

We pick up where we left off
Every time we meet
Weeks, months, years
Concertinaed in an extraordinary feat

Seasons collapse together
In a cascade of exuberant chatter
Miraculously joined as one
Quantum physics rules shatter

Our youthful crazy adventures
Tumble out in a rush
Do you remember when ... ?
Oh how our cheeks flush!

We smile and laugh together
Cry when hearts speak the truth
Reminiscences connect us
With the wonders of youth

We cram a bulging lifetime
Into a few short hours
Drinking in the sensations
Of our childhood-friendship's powers

And then it's all over
Once again we're separate parts
Waiting to discover
What the future for us charts

Yet in our dash to catch-up
Before the window closes
We sense the value
This time-stretching friendship exposes

For as we sit and natter
On distant memories to gorge
An internal fire is replenished
As in a blacksmith's forge

Sparks transform tired souls
When hammer and anvil reunite

That just-like-yesterday feeling
We grasp and hold tight.

END

POETRY WRITING COURSE

"Transforming your ideas into words, and your words into poetry."

Introduction

Aimed mainly at the new and emerging poet, and writers exploring poetry for the first time, packed full of tasks and research points, THE POET's new distance-learning *Poetry Writing Course* takes you through the elements that make amazing poetry, and the skills, methods and techniques you can use to begin exploring poetry for the first time, or to help develop and better your own work.

This Poetry Writing Course focuses on getting you, the student, to practise writing poetry across a wide range of styles, themes and topics.

The learning objectives of this course are:

- To give you a basic knowledge of the history of poetry.
- To recognise and be able to experiment with key poetic structures.
- To understand key poetic terms, techniques and devices, and how to apply them to your own poetry.
- To be able to write in a range of poetic forms.
- To recognise and develop your own style, and demonstrate your own poetic voice in your work.
- To be confident in your use of different poetic techniques such as rhyme, metre and figurative language.
- To be confident in experimenting with your poetry.
- To understand the importance of punctuation in meaning.
- To give you some tips and hints in approaching editors and submitting to publications.
- To understand the differences between finding a commercial publisher and self-publishing your own collection of poetry.

For further information go to:

www.THEPOETmagazine.org

and click on Poetry Writing Course

Compiled and published by:

Robin Barratt Publishing
Affordable Publishing Services

Books, Magazines, Newsletters, Websites.

www.RobinBarratt.co.uk